CHANGING THE BEAT

Lifting Communities with Relevant Policing

Andy Harvey

Dear Reader,

In the midst of an unexpected life storm, unfair and relentless at times, I chose to release this book as a testament to the power of moving forward. In the face of adversity, I've made the conscious decision to progress, and I hope this message serves as both a challenge and an inspiration for you to do the same when life hits you.

ISBN: 979-8-8620-3556-8

DEDICATION

To my children, Samantha, and Jacob, you are my guiding lights and the reason for every endeavor. This book is dedicated to you, a reflection of the values I hold dear. I love you very much.

To my Mom and Dad in Heaven, you raised me to love others and to stand for what's right. I've tried to do both and have the scars to prove it.

To those who've unwaveringly believed in me, your support has been my anchor through adversity. You know who you are.

To former Dallas Police Chief and mentor, David Kunkle, who recently passed away. You impacted many in our profession. This book is a tribute to you. Rest in Eternal Peace, Chief.

To my fellow law enforcement peers, your sacrifices and unwavering commitment are a testament to your strength. May this message serve as a reminder that your service matters, your dedication is felt, and your impact is immeasurable.

CONTENTS

PART IV AUTHORITY, POWER, AND LEGITIMACY

PART V KNOW THYSELF AND EMBRACE OUR HUMANITY

FOREWORD

There is so much more to being a police officer than putting on the uniform. Changing The Beat should be mandatory reading for every law enforcement officer in the United States. Harvey keeps the momentum going from his first book, Excellence in Policing. Every citizen encounter is an opportunity to create and build relationships with your community. The relationships within law enforcement are just as important. Chief Harvey believes in building a culture of wellness within an agency and writes about its importance in the book. As a retired police officer with over 28 years of experience, I wish this information would have been available to me soon.

Ernie Stevens, SAPD (Ret)
HBO's Ernie and Joe: Crisis Cop

In a world where building trust and meaningful connections between police departments and communities is paramount, Harvey offers a compelling reminder that relevance is the key to making a lasting impact. This book serves as a wake-up call for officers and leaders to recognize the importance of their influence to foster positive change. If you are committed to shaping a future where police departments are catalysts for unity, understanding, and transformation, then this is a must read. Changing The Beat is a testament to the ripple effect that relevance can create, and it leaves us with the conviction that by being intentional in our actions, we can sow the seeds of positive change that will resonate for generations to come.

Mike Alexander, Chief of Police (Ret)
Organizational Development Expert

As a young officer, Chief Harvey's first book, Excellence in Policing, was a game-changer, reshaping how I viewed policing. It confronted the traditional ideas within our profession, inspiring a stronger dedication to excellence and community service. Now, with Changing the Beat, the journey of transformation continues. This book goes even further, pushing the boundaries of law enforcement. It challenges us to adapt and to be relevant in an ever-changing world. This book reinforces the essence of policing isn't just about enforcing laws; it's about evolving and using our influence to make a lasting, positive impact on the communities we serve. And this truth remains, "Don't be an a@@hole!"

Ramzey Chiat
Police Officer, North Texas

Your first book, Excellence in Policing, helped broadened my view on policing. And now, "Changing The Beat" builds on your message of excellence by continuing to challenge our belief systems. Andy, I have known you for over a decade and have always admired your genuine and sincere approach to making everyone a better person, to know their worth. You truly care about people, as well as the greater community but more importantly you also possess the unique ability to take what you care about and make it relevant to others, to not only better themselves but also the people around them. One of the pieces of advice that you gave me was to invest in myself by furthering my professional training and academic education. This advice has paid off greatly in both my personal and professional life. Thank you for the meaningful contribution you have made in my life and in the lives of many others.

Vincent Montez, Lieutenant
Bee Cave, Texas Police Department

INTRODUCTION

In 2017, Excellence in Policing was released to help officers across the nation think differently and critically about every police-citizen encounter. Since then, our nation has experienced a series of momentous events that continues to shape the landscape of law enforcement. The deaths of George Floyd, Daunte Wright, and Breonna Taylor sparked widespread protests and profound discussions about the state of policing in our society.

These protests demanded change, calling for a reevaluation of how the police allocate resources and support various community needs. Amidst the turmoil, many dedicated police officers found themselves grappling with feelings of frustration and disillusionment. They felt underappreciated and questioned whether they should continue putting their lives on the line for a society that seemed critical of their every move.

As a result, recruitment and retention became increasingly challenging, leading to staffing shortages in police departments across the nation. Amid public scrutiny, some officers hesitated to engage in proactive policing, fearing unintended consequences. Yet, despite these difficulties, there remained a strong core of unwavering officers like yourself—men and women who continued to bravely serve their communities day in and day out.

Ok, so where do we go from here? How can we continue to build trust and confidence between law enforcement and communities and forge a path towards a brighter future? It is evident that the role of policing has evolved, but still requires a commonsense approach—one that emphasizes mutual respect, understanding, and cooperation.

Fortunately, amidst the challenges, there is still a vast majority of the population that believes in the importance of having a strong, well equipped, and highly trained police force. They recognize the essential role officers play in ensuring public safety and protecting the vulnerable. The heart of policing still lies in every encounter between officers and citizens, providing an opportunity to foster positive relationships and build trust.

This book embarks on a transformative journey, exploring essential elements that can continue to shape the future of policing. We will delve into approaches and strategies that aim to strengthen trust, enhance communication, and promote collaboration between law enforcement and the communities. The challenges we face are not insurmountable. Rather, they serve as opportunities to create lasting change that benefits us all. This is not a passive undertaking—it is a call to action, a chance to take part in shaping the future of law enforcement. By working together, we can strengthen policing, making it a more powerful source of safety and support. Furthermore, those of us in policing have a responsibility to leave our profession better than the way we found it.

"…those of us in policing have a responsibility to leave our profession better than the way we found it."

This book will equip you with additional knowledge and tools to make a difference and contribute to a society where safety, mutual understanding, and mutual respect are at the forefront. The future of policing lies in the hands of those who embrace change and work towards unity. Together, we build a stronger and safer society, driven by a common purpose—to protect, to serve, and to uplift.

Before we embark on this continuous journey, I want to address a misconception that may cloud your perception of this message. Some may see these *soft skills* as a sign of weakness, but it is quite the opposite. Embracing excellence in policing requires not only physical strength but also unwavering mental fortitude.

As a police officer, you represent the embodiment of courage and resilience. You wear the badge with pride, knowing the weight of responsibility it carries. Society places high expectations upon you, often unrealistically so. Disrespect, questioning, relentless scrutiny, and a lack of appreciation may become all too familiar. However, despite these challenges, people still turn to you in their darkest moments because they believe in your ability to make a difference.

So, one thing must be abundantly clear: your goal is to return home safely to your loved ones every night. While you are expected to exercise restraint and uphold peace, you must remember that you are human. You are **not** a punching bag for anyone's abuse! If anyone dares to threaten your safety, you are equipped with the knowledge and strength gained through your training to protect yourself, your fellow officers, and our citizenry. Every encounter should strive to ensure the safety of all involved, but we must acknowledge that we live in a world tainted by violence and dangerous individuals who may seek to harm you.

The principles we will discuss in this book are designed to guide you in policing that uplifts communities and fosters trust and confidence. Most importantly, it emphasizes the safety of both you and others. By adhering to these principles, you will become the best version of yourself, equipped to handle any situation that comes your way. With this understanding firmly established, let's take this path together. Be ready to learn, grow, and become the epitome of policing.

First, let's make sure you are relevant.

PART I

THE POWER OF RELEVANCE

…"protecting and serving in an urban community is much more than crime-fighting; the burden placed on urban police is they have the power to either tear a city apart or help hold it together,"
Officer Brian Willingham, Flint Town, Ep. 2

CHAPTER 1
SILENT SHADOWS: EMBRACE RELEVANCE FOR POSITIVE CHANGE

A 'shadow' group is that part of an organization that is hidden, not widely spoken about, or compared to in an open manner.[i] It is a metaphorical term used to describe a situation where an entity or part of an organization remains unnoticed or unknown, operating in the background without attracting attention or awareness. In other words, they are silent. For our purposes, 'silent shadows,' in the context of policing, refers to law enforcement agencies or departments that lack visibility, relevance, or meaningful engagement with the community.

When a police department remains in the shadows, its impact and efforts may go unnoticed, and the trust and confidence of the community it serves may not be fully established. The term emphasizes the importance of being visible, relevant, and actively engaged in the community, as this presence is crucial for fostering trust, cooperation, and a sense of security among the public.[ii]

In today's policing, the power of relevance has become paramount in the pursuit of effective law enforcement. It hinges upon the realization that a police department's influence extends far beyond maintaining law and order; it holds the potential to uplift an entire community. Being relevant helps with other policing challenges such as recruiting and building trust and confidence in the agency.

People want to be a part of something special. So, when we create an organization that is effectively engaging the community and is innovative, people will be drawn to that. In one of my medium sized police departments, for example, 175 people registered to take the entrance exam. The department had never seen those kinds of numbers. Moreover, 140 people showed up to test. For a medium sized city and in today's current state, this was monumental. I truly believe because of our relevance not only in our city but the region, aspiring and experienced officers noticed and were drawn to our agency. This is the power of relevance.

It's very possible for the police to provide basic services to the community while failing to add value. If the impact of their actions remains unseen and unknown, their efforts to build confidence and trust become inconsequential. In other words, no one cares because no one is paying attention. In any city, the police department wields unparalleled influence, not to minimize the importance of other city departments, but to highlight the unique ability of law enforcement to unite people, foster collaboration, and inspire collective change.

"It's possible for the police to provide basic services to the community while failing to add value."

When a police department intentionally engages their city, a transformative power is unleashed. It creates a force of influencers, ambassadors, and advocates who passionately align themselves with the department's mission. By nurturing these relationships, the department gets out of the shadows and becomes a relevant entity that resonates deeply with its residents.

This section of the book harnesses the power of relevance to effect positive change. It invites you to embark on a journey of discovering how authenticity, consistency, and genuine care can shape a police department into a beacon of relevance and an agent of lasting impact within their communities. When relevant, a police department empowers their community, inspires collective action, and creates an environment where mutual trust and shared responsibility thrive. Is your department a silent shadow in your community?

Let's find out in the next chapter.

CHAPTER 2
WHAT IS R.EL.E.V.A.N.T. POLICING?

Now, let's explore the essence of R.E.L.E.V.A.N.T policing and discover what characteristics define a relevant police department.

R- RELATIONSHIP BUILDERS

Building strong relationships between law enforcement and community members lies at the heart of community policing. The R in community policing stands for Relationship-Building, emphasizing the critical nature of fostering positive connections. Trust, open communication, and mutual respect form the foundation for effective collaboration. By establishing trust, law enforcement officers can bridge the gap between themselves and the community, creating an environment where citizens feel comfortable assistance and sharing vital information with the police.

Open communication channels promote transparency and understanding, enabling officers to gain valuable insights into community concerns and needs. Mutual respect ensures that interactions are conducted with dignity and fairness, reinforcing the notion that law enforcement and community members are partners. Through Relationship-Building, community policing cultivates a shared sense of responsibility and creates force multipliers where collaboration flourishes, fostering safer and stronger communities.

E- EXCELLENCE DRIVEN

The E in community policing represents Excellence, a core principle that guides its endeavors. Excellence driven policing is dedicated to upholding high professional standards and continuously striving for improvement. It recognizes that excellence is not a static achievement but an ongoing pursuit. By setting high expectations and standards, law enforcement agencies engaged in community policing commit to delivering quality services to the community they serve.

This commitment extends beyond mere enforcement; it encompasses proactive problem-solving, timely responsiveness to community needs, thus, fostering a safe and inclusive environment. Through a culture of excellence, policing seeks to exceed expectations, rapidly adapt to evolving challenges, and consistently provide the highest level of service to the community. It is through this unwavering pursuit of excellence that community policing reinforces its commitment to creating safer, more resilient communities for all.

L- LOCAL FOCUS

The L in community policing emphasizes Local Focus, recognizing the significance of addressing the distinct needs of individual neighborhoods and areas. Community policing understands that every community, even neighborhoods, possesses unique characteristics, challenges, and dynamics that must be considered. It goes beyond a one-size-fits-all approach and delves into the specific context of each community. By actively listening and engaging with community members, law enforcement gains a deep understanding of the issues that impact their daily lives. These quality-of-life issues enables the development and implementation of targeted strategies that address the specific concerns and priorities of each community. This emphasizes to citizens that we are listening and are all in.

Whether it's enhancing community relations, reducing localized crime, or improving quality of life, community policing seeks to tailor its efforts to effectively meet the diverse needs of the neighborhoods it serves. By embracing Local Focus, community policing empowers communities, fostering collaboration and generating positive outcomes that resonate on a local level.

E- EMPOWERMED COMMUNITIES

The E in community policing stands for Empowerment, highlighting its commitment to involving community members in decision-making processes, problem-solving, and crime prevention efforts. Community policing recognizes that empowering individuals and community organizations is essential for fostering a sense of ownership and shared responsibility for public safety. By actively engaging and collaborating with the community, law enforcement agencies create opportunities for community members to have a seat at the table; a voice in shaping policies and strategies that affect them directly. This involvement not only enhances the effectiveness of policing initiatives but also builds trust, strengthens relationships, and nurtures a sense of belonging within the community.

Empowered community members become active participants in crime prevention, equipped with the knowledge, resources, and support to address local concerns. Through Empowerment, community policing fosters a culture of shared responsibility, enabling community members to take an active role in creating safer and more resilient neighborhoods.

V- VISIBLE PRESENCE

The V in community policing represents Visibility, which is a fundamental aspect of its approach. Community policing recognizes the importance of maintaining a visible police presence in the community. Regular patrols, including on foot, bikes, motorcycles, and even mounted patrols can contribute to crime reductions by creating a sense of vigilance and awareness. Visible law enforcement officers act as a deterrent to potential offenders, signaling a proactive and responsive approach to public safety. High visibility makes people feel safer, an important factor in measuring success.

Visibility also serves to build trust and foster positive relationships with community members. Interactions between law enforcement officers and community members, whether during patrols, community events, or informal conversations, help to bridge the gap between law enforcement and the community. By being accessible and approachable, officers can engage in meaningful dialogue, listen to community concerns, and establish a sense of familiarity and connection.

Maintaining visibility also plays a vital role in fostering a sense of security within the community. When community members see law enforcement actively present and engaged, they gain confidence and reassurance, knowing that their safety is being prioritized. A visible police presence can help alleviate fear and contribute to a positive perception of safety, enhancing the overall quality of life for residents.

A-ACCOUNTABILITY

The A in community policing signifies Accountability, a cornerstone of its philosophy. Community policing places a strong emphasis on accountability for both law enforcement agencies and community members alike. Police departments strive to be accountable to the community they serve by prioritizing transparency, responsiveness, and fairness in their operations. This entails maintaining open lines of communication, actively seeking community input, and ensuring that policies and practices align with community values and needs.

By being transparent about decision-making processes and actively addressing concerns, law enforcement agencies build trust and foster a collaborative relationship with the community. True transparency includes being open about the good, the bad, and yes, the ugly.

Simultaneously, community members are encouraged to take responsibility for their neighborhoods and actively engage in partnership with the police. This means being vigilant, reporting suspicious activities, and working collaboratively to prevent and address crime. By assuming a proactive role, community members become stakeholders in their own safety, contributing to the overall well-being of their neighborhoods. When both law enforcement and community members uphold their respective responsibilities, a culture of mutual accountability is fostered, creating a foundation for effective crime prevention and a sense of shared ownership in community policing efforts.

Through Accountability, community policing promotes a partnership built on trust, fairness, and collective responsibility. It reinforces the notion that safety and security are shared endeavors, requiring the active participation and accountability of both law enforcement and communities.

N- NEEDS BASED

Relevant community policing focuses on addressing the specific needs and priorities of the community. It involves conducting thorough assessments of community concerns, analyzing data, and tailoring strategies to effectively respond to those needs.

Community policing begins by conducting thorough assessments of community concerns. This includes actively listening to community members, conducting surveys, and engaging in dialogue to gather insights into the specific issues they face. It also involves analyzing relevant data, such as crime statistics and trends, to identify patterns and areas of focus.

Armed with this information, community policing tailors its strategies and initiatives to effectively respond to the identified needs. This may involve the implementation of targeted programs, initiatives, and partnerships that address the root causes of community concerns. By focusing on the specific needs of the community, community policing maximizes its impact, ensuring that resources are allocated where they are most needed.

When I served as the police chief in Palestine, Texas, we launched a program named Unidos en Palestine (United in Palestine) to connect and engage with Spanish speaking community. The goal was to build trust in the police among all members of the Palestine community. We realized their needed to be a way to communicate more effectively about program events and other information with the multicultural community.

We decided that Facebook would be the best platform, since this was the most popular at the time. So, the department created a Facebook page for Unidos en Palestine, and in three days gained more than 1,000 followers and continued to grow. The Facebook page provided pertinent and relevant information other than just crime related matters. The page included information such as school closings, inclement weather warnings, power outages, and notices from the city government.

In addition, community members could post information about their community events, job opportunities, calls for volunteers to help with community projects, local sports news, reports of missing dogs, and a wide variety of other matters. The Police Department also used the Facebook account to provide information to community members, in their own language, on routine matters like how to get car insurance or pay a water bill; the kind of information most may take for granted.

Unidos en Palestine also held biweekly meetings in police training rooms, where members of the community, police officers, and community leaders met to discuss local issues. This was a game changer for how the police department was able to earn trust from a segment of the community that may have felt minimized or neglected.

The needs-based approach also promotes a sense of inclusivity and collaboration within the community. Community members feel heard and valued when their concerns are addressed, fostering a stronger sense of trust and engagement between law enforcement and the community. This collaborative effort helps to create sustainable and impactful solutions to community challenges.

Through a needs-based approach, community policing ensures that its efforts are responsive, relevant, and directly aligned with the needs and priorities of the community. By addressing these specific needs, community policing fosters a more resilient community.

T- TRUST BUILDERS

Relevance signifies Trust-Building, which is the foundational element of policing. Community policing recognizes that trust between law enforcement and community members is essential for effective collaboration and successful crime prevention efforts.

Trust is established through consistent, respectful, and fair interactions between law enforcement officers and community members. This involves treating individuals with dignity and respect, actively listening to their concerns, and valuing their perspectives. Law enforcement officers engage in positive interactions, demonstrating empathy, understanding, and cultural sensitivity to build bridges of trust within the community. The tenets of procedural justice will be discussed in a later chapter.

Moreover, trust is nurtured by delivering on commitments. Therefore, it is important to manage expectations. Be sure and under promise and over deliver. Be realistic with the community about the police department's true capabilities. Relevant law enforcement agencies work diligently to satisfy citizen expectations, whether it's implementing community-driven initiatives, responding promptly to reported concerns, or providing regular updates on progress. Consistency and follow-through in actions reinforce the credibility of law enforcement and build confidence in their ability to address community needs.

Transparency and accountability further contribute to trust-building. Community policing emphasizes open communication, sharing information, and involving community members in decision-making processes. By fostering transparency, law enforcement agencies demonstrate their commitment to fair and just practices, instilling confidence in the community.

Ultimately, trust-building in community policing creates a positive cycle. As trust increases, community members become more willing to collaborate, share information, and actively participate in crime prevention efforts. This collaborative relationship strengthens the effectiveness of community policing initiatives, enabling law enforcement and community members to work together towards shared goals.

In conclusion, by capitalizing on the unique influence of police departments have in lifting communities, let's recognize that your impact extends far beyond traditional enforcement duties. Through Relationship-Building, Excellence, Local

Focus, Empowerment, Visibility, Accountability, Needs-Based approaches, and Trust-Building, relevant policing cultivates an environment of collaboration and shared responsibility. By authentically and consistently serving their communities, law enforcement agencies can create an army of advocates who passionately endorse their brand and contribute to their relevancy.

Based on the tenets of R.E.L.E.V.A.N.T policing, how would you grade your police department?

CHAPTER 3
POLICING BEYOND NUMBERS

Numbers. They hold a certain allure. Statistics? Even more so, especially in measuring our success. "Let's assess our performance," says the police chief. "Violent crimes down by 7%, but property crimes increased by 13%. What's happening in your district, Captain Usuck? How many arrests last week? Citations issued? Drugs recovered?" Captain, "Well, my officers have been active on the streets- they made 45 arrests, 148 traffic stops, issued 128 citations, and cleared 8 offenses." Chief responds, "Not good enough. Your property crimes are up, and I expect them to be down next week."

If you've sat in a CompStat-type meeting, this sounds familiar. It's all about the numbers and bringing crime down. Do whatever it takes—use overtime if necessary. Repeat the process next week, same report, same response, and hopefully different results.

Since the mid-1990s through the 2000s, crime steadily decreased in our country. Police chiefs and mayors annually celebrated declining crime rates. "Crime is down for the 5th straight year. Our proactive crime strategies are effective once again." Blah, blah, blah. There's nothing wrong with celebrating less crime, even if it's on paper only. Or is it?

Crime is down—good news. But at what cost? Specifically, how do those numbers impact the health and quality of life in neighborhoods under police scrutiny? More importantly, do they erode trust and confidence in the police department? It can be a slippery slope if not monitored closely.

Policing by numbers solely can be redundant, non-effective, and at times, counterproductive. Numbers matter, and we should use them to analyze crime patterns cautiously and respond accordingly. Conversely, when policing is solely driven by numbers, any numbers, in the end that's all we have. Have you ever considered that lower crime doesn't always make people feel safer or improve their perception of your department?

Here's the point- When we focus on quality actions, the right numbers follow. Numbers without impact are meaningless. Quality, however, is the key—actions taken by officers that add value to the community and its spirit.

PART II

THE AGILE POLICE OFFICER

"Agile minded officers learn how to adapt, embrace change, and continuously improve their skills and strategies during every police-citizen encounter."

CHAPTER 4
THE CHEETAH'S MOST POWERFUL TOOL- AGILE MINDSET

In the vast expanse of the African savannas, a remarkable predator reigns as the fastest land animal on Earth - the cheetah. Known for its breathtaking speed, this graceful feline teaches us a valuable lesson about adaptability and agility. Interestingly, research by biochemist Alan Wilson unveils that a cheetah's exceptional hunting success does not solely depend on its unmatched speed.[iii] Instead, cheetahs thrive by demonstrating an agile mindset and physical prowess, swiftly changing direction, and pace during its pursuit of prey, and its hunting strategy.

This captivating revelation by Wilson and his team offers profound insights into how animals operate and thrive in their natural environment. Equipped with sophisticated radio collars, these researchers monitored the cheetahs with unprecedented precision, gathering real-world data on their hunting techniques. To their surprise, the cheetahs did not always sprint at full speed but, rather, strategically slowed down in specific strides to outmaneuver their prey. This ability to decelerate and turn quickly is crucial for their hunting success, showcasing the essence of agility.

Having an agile approach in policing, like the cheetah's adaptive hunting skills, is about utilizing more than solely your strongest skill, it's embracing change and acting decisively. An agile police officer doesn't solely rely on the authority of the badge but utilizes his mind as the most important weapon in his arsenal.

As we delve into the concept of agile policing, we will explore how its practices mirror the cheetah's agile mindset. By harnessing the power of adaptability, collaboration, and continuous improvement, you can become more agile, navigating the challenges of modern policing with swiftness, precision, and confidence.

Agile is a term in the private sector that is used to describe a type of project management approach that is characterized by flexibility, collaboration, and rapid duplication. The agile mindset is a thought process that involves understanding, collaborating, learning, and staying flexible to achieve high-performing results.[iv] Agile methods are designed to help teams respond quickly to changing circumstances and customer needs and are often used in software development and other types of projects where flexibility and adaptability are key.

Agile approaches are based on a set of values and principles outlined in the Agile Manifesto, discussed in the next chapter, that emphasize the importance of delivering working software quickly, responding to change, and collaborating with customers and team members. Although this manifesto was created for the private sector, many of its principles can be applied to improve our profession.

Since everything begins in the mind, how and what we think is critical in achieving our goals. In today's rapidly changing law enforcement landscape, the need for adaptability, efficiency, and effective problem-solving has never been greater. As an agile-minded officer, you will be equipped with more critical thinking tools to tackle the challenges and complexities of modern policing.

Just as the concept of being agile has revolutionized various private industries, it's principles can also help the public sector. Agile minded officers learn how to adapt, embrace change, and continuously improve their skills and strategies during every police-citizen encounter. Being agile is another way of achieving excellence. Webster's definition of agile is marked by ready ability to move quick, easy, grace like an agile dancer, and having a quick resourceful and adaptive character, as having an agile mind.[v]

According to the Agile Alliance, "Agile is the ability to create and respond to change. It is a way of dealing with, and ultimately succeeding in, an uncertain and turbulent environment."[vi] Adaptability is essential for law enforcement professionals. The threats to public safety and society's expectations keep evolving, so our profession must do the same. An agile mindset, which values flexibility and quick responses to change, including calling audibles in the field, if necessary, can help police officers thrive amid these challenges.

An agile mindset can provide numerous benefits for police officers. Some of the key benefits include:

The ability to respond quickly and effectively to changing circumstances: In an agile mindset, the focus is on adapting to change and continuously improving processes. This can be particularly useful for police officers, who often face unexpected challenges and must make decisions in both routine and high-pressure situations.

Improved communication and collaboration: Agile approaches place a strong emphasis on collaboration and transparency. This can help police officers work more effectively as a team and improve communication with colleagues, supervisors, and the community.

Greater customer satisfaction: In the case of policing, the "customer" is the community being served. By adopting an agile mindset, police officers can be more responsive to the needs and concerns of the community, leading to greater satisfaction and trust.

CHAPTER 5
THE AGILE MANIFESTO TAKE-AWAYS FOR POLICING

The Agile Manifesto is a set of values and principles that guide the development and delivery of complex products and services. It was created in 2001 by a group of software developers who were seeking a better way to manage projects and deliver value to customers; they lost sight of what really mattered—pleasing their customers.[vii] The Agile Manifesto consists of four values and twelve principles.

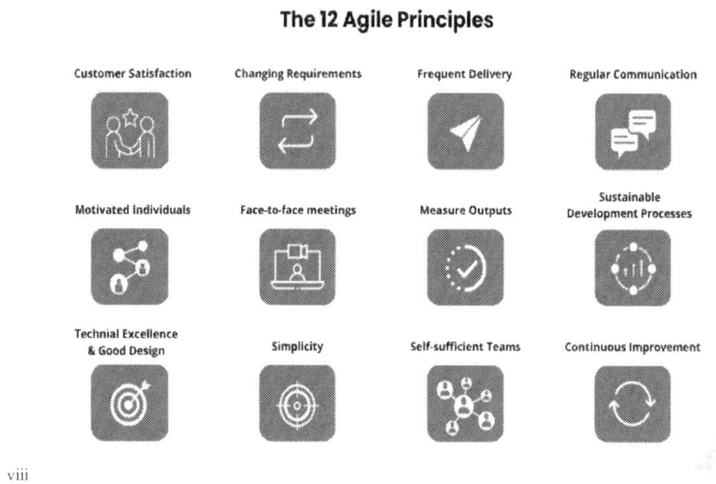

The Agile Manifesto's values are designed to help teams deliver value to customers quickly and effectively, and they can be applied in many different fields, including policing. Some ways the principles of the Agile Manifesto could be applied to policing include:

Prioritizing Customer Satisfaction In policing, the "customer" is everyone you encounter in the community being served. By prioritizing the needs and concerns of the community, police officers can build trust and deliver value to the people they serve. Some examples of a customer-centric approach both police officers and departments may include:

Community Policing Initiatives: Police departments frequently set up community policing units or initiatives. To better understand the needs and problems of the community, officers in these units interact often with residents, attend community meetings, and engage in meaningful conversation. For instance, to answer people' concerns about safety, officers may set up neighborhood watch programs.

Community Outreach Programs: Police departments organize community events, workshops, and meetings to actively engage with residents. These events address concerns, share information, and build relationships, putting the community's needs at the forefront.

Police may focus on topics such as crime prevention that are specific to the issues of various communities. These interactions indicate that the police are attentive to the community's requirements for safety while also giving locals useful information.

Crisis Intervention: In cases involving mental health crises, crisis intervention-trained cops concentrate on de-escalation and making sure the person receiving care is receiving the proper attention. The welfare of community members who are in need is given priority in this strategy.

Conflict Resolution: Officers may participate in community conflict resolution initiatives, mediating conflicts to stop them from developing into criminal events. This proactive strategy addresses neighborhood issues before they develop into more serious problems.

Surveys: Police departments may undertake community surveys or host town hall meetings to get feedback from the local population. Asking about safety issues or seeking suggestions for enhancing police-community ties are just a few examples of possible questions. Policing tactics are shaped by this input.

Responsive Policing: Police that respond urgently to community complaints are said to practice responsive policing. For instance, if burglaries in the community increase, the police step up patrols and collaborate closely with locals to create crime prevention plans and act on them quickly.

School Resource Officers: Officers assigned to schools prioritize the safety and well-being of students. They mentor and educate students on various topics, reinforcing the idea that the community's youth are valuable members deserving of respect and support.

Victim-Centered Approaches: In cases of crime, officers aim to support victims by providing information, resources, and emotional assistance. This approach emphasizes that the community's well-being matters.

Cultural Competency Training: Police officers are given training in cultural competency so they can respect and comprehend the various cultures present in their community. Officers are better able to communicate and respond to the requirements of various groups because to this.

Public Safety Changing Requirements To effectively serve and protect their communities, police officers must be able to adapt their plans and tactics to the changing nature of crime and threats to public safety. Officers that have an agile mindset are better able to adapt to change and refine their enforcement methods over time.

Drug Enforcement Strategies: Police adjust their enforcement tactics in response to shifting drug trends. For instance, the opioid crisis necessitated a change in strategy, which included making naloxone (Narcan) more widely available for use in overdose reversal and focusing on drug traffickers rather than low-level users.

Body-Worn Cameras: To increase accountability and transparency, most police departments have implemented body-worn cameras. They make ongoing improvements to the policies and processes relating to the use of cameras to comply with statutory obligations and community expectations. If your department does not have BWC's, you're outdated.

Social Media Engagement: Police agencies understand the value of interacting with the public on social media. They adapt by utilizing social media sites like Twitter and Facebook to exchange information, resolve issues, and forge connections. This flexible application of technology improves community engagement. What social media platform is most of your community is using? Your department needs to be there too.

Crisis Response Training: As active shooter situations have increased, the emphasis on quick deployment and interaction with the threat has changed. Specialized training is provided to police personnel so they can modify their strategies and save lives in these dire circumstances.

Teaming Up With Community Agile methodologies strongly emphasize teamwork, which can be particularly helpful in policing, where strong community ties and communication are essential. Transparency is the best approach to establish trust, and face-to-face contact is the most efficient way to do this. Here are a few examples:

Community Walks: Police officers can stroll or ride a bicycle through neighborhoods, interacting with locals in a friendly and informal way. In addition to fostering great relationships, this makes cops more approachable and visible.

School Visits: Officers connect with students, instructors, and parents during visits to local schools. By establishing ties with children through visits to their schools, police enforcement is more likely to be viewed favorably from an early age.

Coffee/Haircut with a Cop: These events may seem insignificant, but I can guarantee you that the public sees its police force engaging with them. Organize informal get-togethers in local coffee shops or barber shops (or any other establishment where people meet- be creative!) so that residents can chat with police officers while enjoying a cup of coffee. These informal settings encourage open dialogue and connections are established.

Neighborhood Policing: Create a community policing strategy by assigning police to particular communities. These officers become well-known figures in the neighborhoods, participating in block gatherings and attending to local issues.

Community Policing Academies: Host community policing academies so that locals can gain knowledge of the practices, regulations, and daily activities of the police. These initiatives support openness and education. Host academies in other languages. This goes a long way for the non-English speaking communities. Furthermore, they will serve as your ambassadors, especially in times of crisis.

Local Events Participation: Actively participate in local events, fairs, and festivals. Set up booths or information centers to engage with the community, answer questions, and provide resources.

Ride-Alongs: Offer community members the opportunity to participate in ride-alongs with officers. This allows residents to experience a day in the life of a police officer and gain a better understanding of their roles and challenges. Don't be afraid to invite the beat reporters. These relationships can help promote the department positively and may contribute to a fairer reporting of critical issues or events.

Motivated Officers As a chief, I search for the unique strengths of both our sworn and non-sworn employees. This made it easier when placing the right people, on the right seat, and on the right bus. I've discovered that when this is achieved, motivation and acceleration occur. Another win-win.

Undoubtedly, the following are some ways how police agencies can develop initiatives around motivated personnel to foster a favorable and encouraging culture:

Community Outreach Projects: Identify police officers who are enthusiastic about community involvement and give them the authority to oversee outreach initiatives. These officers can plan community events, youth mentoring programs, or neighborhood clean-ups to improve relations between the police and the community.

Mental Health Units: Officers with a keen interest in mental health and crisis intervention should be recognized by mental health response teams. To deal to crisis situations involving people with mental illness, put together specific teams of motivated police who undergo additional training in de-escalation tactics and collaborate with mental health specialists.

Youth Engagement: Encourage motivated officers with a heart for young people to create and oversee youth-focused activities with the help of youth engagement programs. These initiatives could consist of after-school activities, instructional workshops, or sports leagues.

Training and Development: Provide ambitious officers with the chance to add value to the department as trainers or instructors. They can organize training sessions on subjects they are enthusiastic about, sharing their knowledge with other officers and enhancing the knowledge and abilities of the entire department.

Problem Solvers: Establish problem-solving teams made up of police who enjoy tackling challenging neighborhood problems. These teams can collaborate with neighborhood partners to identify novel solutions to persistent issues like drug-related violence, homelessness, or traffic safety.

Innovation and Technology Teams: Teams focusing on applying cutting-edge technologies or data-driven strategies to improve enforcement effectiveness and efficiency can capitalize on officers' enthusiasm in technology and innovation. Use your geeks (hey I love geeks) in ways to help you become more efficient and effective for crime fighting.

Simplicity Making the people and their safety your top priority means embracing simplicity. It entails eliminating pointless red tape and putting an emphasis on effective communication, sensible policing techniques, and community involvement. Officers and agencies can better serve the needs of their community and establish trust and productive relationships when they streamline their procedures.

Ensure that the police department's lines of communication are open to the public. Try to solve community problems as modestly as you can. Use common sense! Find a way to keep things simple rather than making them more difficult.

Overall, the adoption of agile practices in policing has the potential to positively impact police culture, and can help police departments be more efficient, effective, and responsive to the needs of the community. However, a police department will not reach its full potential unless those in leadership embrace and display agile values.

Remember K.I.S.S? Keep it simple.

Not this KISS

D 20659189 © Mario Beauregard| Dreamstime.

CHAPTER 6
5 P'S- CONSIDERATIONS FOR NEW PROGRAM SUCCESS

In this chapter, we're diving into some considerations for making new programs excel in your organization. It's all about the 5 P's – Plan, People, Passion, Partnerships, and Priority. This chapter will help you navigate through the process of implementing a new program. From keeping plans simple, picking the right folks, getting everyone excited, teaming up with others, to making sure your program is a big deal, each P is super important for making things work.

PLAN: Creating a plan is important for any new program, but you don't have to stress about planning every little thing. If you try to figure out every tiny detail, you might never get started! So, make a simple plan, start somewhere, and then be ready to pivot as you learn what works for your city. On another note, your program may not be the best fit for your community and that's okay. Just acknowledge it and do away with it. You gave it a shot. Then it's time to move on to the next one. Remember, this is all part of the journey.

PEOPLE: Adhering to the "who first, then what" principle from the Good to Great framework underscores the importance of selecting individuals with the appropriate mindset and dedication. The success of a program or unit is inherently linked to the caliber of individuals involved. The recruitment process should not shy away from considering less tenured officers, emphasizing strengths relevant to the program's objectives. Doing so will accelerate you achieving your goals. In units like the mental health unit, for example, priority should be given to identifying individuals with the necessary attitude and skills, with minimal focus on weaknesses unless they significantly impact the unit.

PASSION: Passion assumes a central role in specialized units, particularly those addressing specific societal needs such as a youth program or a community outreach unit. Individuals within the unit, from leadership to frontline staff, must demonstrate a profound commitment to the mission, fostering an all-encompassing approach. Passion serves as the driving force behind sustained commitment, innovation, and the adoption of a people-centered approach to policing.

PARTNERSHIPS: Establishing collaborative partnerships with municipal departments, external organizations, community groups, and stakeholders is foundational. Such collaborations amplify resources, facilitate expertise exchange, and contribute to the creation of a more comprehensive and effective support system. Collaborative efforts are well-received, contributing to heightened community awareness and empowerment, thereby influencing the confidence entrusted in the department.

PRIORITY: Elevating programs to a position of priority within the broader policing strategy and community is imperative. These should never be a "check the box" decision. The implementation of new programs should surpass an obligatory checklist approach. Adequate allocation of financial and human resources is non-negotiable. Wholehearted belief and commitment are prerequisites for success, as half-hearted endeavors may yield counterproductive results for both the individual and the department.

CHAPTER 7
AGILE LEADERS BUILD STRONG TEAMS AND CULTURE

Leaders serve as the driving force behind the implementation of agile practices and principles within their teams and organizations. When leaders display agile values, they create a strong example for their team members, pushing them to embrace these values in their work as well. This fosters greater trust in the workplace. And without trust, no one will follow you. Agile leaders can build strong agile teams and culture by doing the following:

Encourage open and honest communication: Agile teams rely on open and honest communication; therefore, leaders must create a secure and supportive environment in which team members feel comfortable sharing their thoughts and ideas. Again, face-to-face communication is the most efficient and effective technique of imparting information to a team. Do not be a withholder of information. This breeds rumors and misinformation that can be cancerous to any team or organization. Agile leaders should be open and transparent with information, and they should endeavor to keep team members informed about the team's progress and direction.

Leading by example: Agile leaders should model the behaviors and values that they want to see in the team, including honesty, transparency, and collaboration. Always display your willingness to be open to adapting to change. Your people must see you practicing what you are asking them to do.

"It's not do as you say, because they will do what you do!"

Agile leaders embrace change and encourage their teams to be flexible and responsive to evolving circumstances. Their ability to adapt quickly to new information or shifting priorities empowers the team to make necessary adjustments and deliver value to customers efficiently. Remember the scene in Saving Private Ryan? Gripes go up, not down- never complain in front of your troops. Moreover, this also means praise goes down. Lift your people every chance you get.

Equip your people: Agile leaders should provide the team with the support and resources they need to be successful and should be available to address any issues or concerns that may arise. Leaders, this means speaking up for your people. Do not remain silent but be diplomatic about how you do it. It's important for your people to see that you are supporting them, even if you don't always get what you ask for. There are few things more discouraging than not being equipped properly to do your job effectively.

Recognizing and rewarding good work: Leadership 101. Agile leaders should recognize and reward good work and should show appreciation for the contributions of team members. The best way is to always praise your people publicly. There are moments every day to reinforce positive behavior, you just must look for them. Officers may say they don't do this for the recognition, but when it happens, they appreciate it very much. Be an encourager!

Continuous Improvement: Agile leaders are committed to learning and growing, both individually and as a team. They encourage a culture of continuous improvement, where team members regularly reflect on their processes and practices and seek ways to enhance performance and outcomes. Remember, continuously striving for improvement is the definition of excellence. And don't forget- Listen to your people.

Provide opportunities for team members to contribute: Agile leaders should encourage team members to take ownership of their work and to contribute their skills and expertise to the team. In other words, get the hell out of the way. Do not micromanage! Let your people work and even make mistakes. They will respect and appreciate you more than you realize. In the end, they will make you better!

Leaders who embrace and exemplify agile values are essential for creating a thriving agile environment. Their commitment to transparency, honest communication, adaptability, continuous improvement, and ownership, not only guides their team's success but also helps in building a sustainable and innovative organizational culture.

As agile practices continue in fields such as software development and project management, they can also play an increasing role in the public sector. Agile practices offer several benefits to police departments, including the ability to respond quickly to changing needs, and to continuously improve to better serve their communities. Be like the cheetah.

PART III

MASTERING EVERY POLICE-CITIZEN ENCOUNTER

"Wearing the uniform doesn't set us apart from the community; rather, it makes us more a part of it."

CHAPTER 8
PURSUING EXCELLENCE IN POLICING

Imagine this: a world where everything is marked by extraordinary, class, fineness, brilliance, distinction, greatness, high worth, and quality. Sounds impressive, right? Now, let's take a turn and think about policing. Picture service, duty, authority, strength, honor, commitment, and justice. It's quite a picture, isn't it? But here's the thing – these two seemingly different worlds, excellence and policing, aren't that far apart. In fact, they're deeply connected in ways that can make a meaningful impact on your life and the lives of those you serve.

"A commitment to excellence separates goodness from greatness."

You know what excellence is, right? It's not just a word; it's a mindset, a way of life, a deliberate choice. It's all about pouring in relentless effort, honing a laser focus, and diving deep into the details. It separates the good from the great. And on the flip side, there's mediocrity, the land of "good enough" and "just okay." But hold up – today's policing demands way more than just "okay." If we're talking about moving forward, about stepping up the game, then mediocrity just doesn't cut it.

Bet you're nodding away agreeing because you wouldn't be here if you didn't value excellence. And honestly, with the role policing plays in our nation, being anything less than excellent just doesn't cut it. Mediocrity? Nah, that's not welcome here. People are depending on you – yes, you – to bring your A-game, to be excellent.

But let's clear something up – I'm not talking perfection. Nope, perfection is like chasing a unicorn – you'll never catch one. But you know what the legendary Vince Lombardi said? "Perfection is not attainable, but if we chase perfection, we can catch excellence."[ix] It's like aiming for the bullseye, zeroing in on your target, and giving it your all. Policing isn't a perfect science; dealing with human beings never will be. Mistakes will happen, sure, but excellence means we don't stop there. It means we learn, adapt, and grow, both as individuals and as a profession.

A culture of excellence is powerful. For example, one of the United States Air Force values is- **"EXCELLENCE IN ALL WE DO."** Yes, I bleed blue, what can I say? Excellence is woven into the culture, and guess what? It's no coincidence that they're regarded as the best air force in the world, period. They're all about aiming for excellence, not just in some things, but in all things.

Ask any airman – from the top brass to the fresh recruits – and they'll tell you all about these core values. It's like breathing for them. Imagine if our military was just average and how that would affect our nation, our world. The same principle applies to law enforcement. Your influence on our nation is massive, and people expect nothing less than the very best from you. They're relying on you to be excellent.

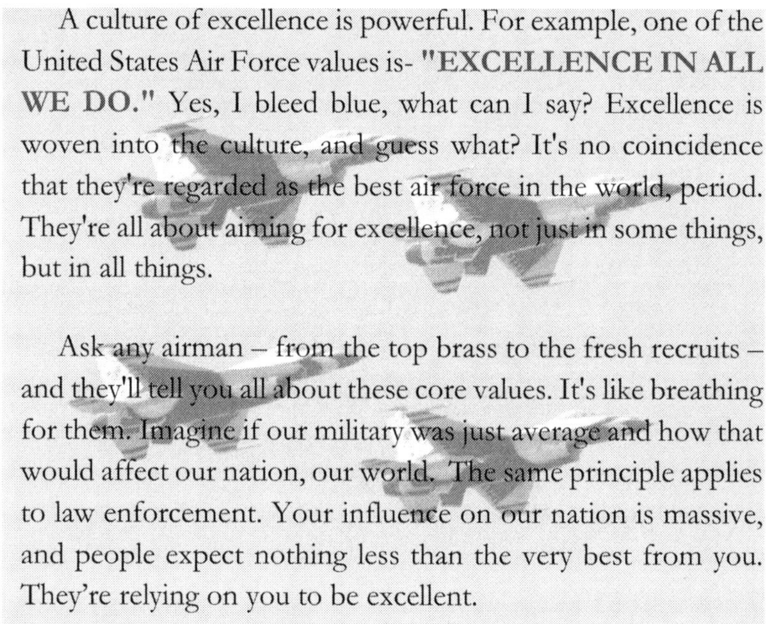

ID125271912 © Aimedon | Dreamstime.com

So, strive for excellence, it is attainable. It's something you can grab hold of and can integrate into your every move. It's about setting the bar high and saying, "I'm going to meet that bar and then some." It's about understanding that while perfection might be out of reach, excellence is well within your grasp. And most importantly, it's about recognizing that your role in policing carries immense weight, and the expectation of excellence isn't just a suggestion – it's a responsibility, and it's yours to own.

CHAPTER 9
EMBRACE CHANGE

Hey, let's get real here. We've hit some high notes on various fronts. But and this is a big but, what got us here won't necessarily get us to the next level. It's time for a shift – a culture of excellence should be our new north star. From rookies to chiefs, every single officer in your department should be gunning for 'Excellence in All You Do.' This isn't just some fancy tagline; it's the spark that will keep us not just relevant on a national stage, but also help us retain our spot as the world's finest.

"What got us to this level of success will not take us to the next one. Policing should build a culture of excellence.

Now, don't get me wrong, celebrating successes is a good thing. But here's the kicker: if we start cozying up to our perceived successes and don't capitalize on that momentum, policing is going to suffer. This principle isn't just about individuals; it happens to organizations too. Once we hit a certain level of achievement, we become too comfortable and feel like everything is fine. But guess what? That's when the danger creeps in – complacency. Before you know it, we're sliding down a slope we never meant to be on. And we can't let that happen, not to our profession, not to our nation.

Policing has had a good run since the mid-1990s. Crime rates dropping across the country have been kind to us. There's even a whole term for it – "The Great American Crime Decline," as coined by Frank Zimring in his book.[x] And trust me, you should give that book a read. It'll challenge your belief systems about crime causations and strategies that have seemingly worked. But hey, there's a twist. While these successes might be good politically, they could turn into our downfall if we don't stay sharp. We've got to act now, before complacency sets in.

Excellence isn't about coasting; it's about eternally aiming for better. Sitting still and hoping for change? That's not just insane; it's downright foolish. Yeah, I said it, foolish! And we're better than that – way better. Settling isn't an option if we want to level up.

Here's the deal – excellence demands change, and we all know cops don't always jump for joy when change is on the menu. Maybe "hate" is too strong a word, but let's be honest, we're not the most change-loving bunch. But here's the reality: reaching for excellence means we must embrace change. Society's evolving at lightning speed, and if we don't keep up, we'll become outdated and more of a hindrance than progressive. Our nation craves excellence.

Now, I won't sugarcoat it – striving for excellence won't be a cake walk. It'll be tough, so brace yourself. One biblical version describes progressing as *straining forward* to reach a goal.[xi] I thought about the word strain and had to look it up. Strain means pain, like what happens when a muscle is overused. The muscle becomes enlarged when it's used in an uncommon way, which results in pain.

Striving for excellence will also cause pain because you will use 'muscles' that you don't use often. But just as the athlete who wants to be the very best, you will have to endure some pain to achieve excellence in all you do. No pain, no gain! Oh, I heard a comedian say it differently, for him he preferred – "no pain, no pain!" Funny, right? But the truth is, nothing valuable comes without sweat and sacrifice. And what you do as a police officer? It's significant, and it's worth every bit of the journey.

CHAPTER 10
CULTIVATING POWERFUL HABITS

Excellence isn't something we're born with. It's a journey of transformation, much like the path of becoming a leader. You weren't gifted excellence from the start – although your parents may disagree. Aristotle, that wise mind from history, said this: " We are what we repeatedly do. Excellence, then, is not an act but a habit."[xii] We don't do things rightly because we possess virtue or excellence; rather, we have those because we've done things rightly. We are what we consistently do. Excellence isn't just a show; it's a habit.

"Excellence, then, is not an act, but a habit." Aristotle

Habits – they're the building blocks of our lives. Simply put, they're things we do repeatedly. However, if you're not cautious, you can unknowingly develop not-so-great habits in policing. And let's be real – kicking those bad habit is way tougher than establishing healthy ones.

If you're aiming for excellence in policing, it's time to get brutally honest about where you're at now. That means acknowledging that you might've bought into or learned some false beliefs along the way, beliefs that have cunningly disguised themselves as truths.

Yes, there'll be hiccups. There'll be days when your excellence game will not be on point. But guess what? That's just a little detour on the road to improvement. Again – we're all human, and perfection isn't the aim. Excellence is about always striving to raise the bar, even in the face of failure. When we mess up – and trust me, we will – the key is to own it, learn from it, and then move forward with determination. It's seizing the next opportunity to show excellence, to shine.

ID69917306 © Mrchan |Dreamstime.com

So, here's the takeaway: excellence isn't a grand event. It's the small steps you take every single day. It's those seemingly minor choices that collectively create a pattern of excellence. And yes, it's a journey; you'll grow, stumble, learn, and ultimately, become excellent in all you do.

CHAPTER 11
CONFRONT THE UNCOMFORTABLE

Achieving excellence demands that you step out of your cozy comfort zone. Jim Collins, in his book "Good to Great," wrote about the Stockdale Paradox. It goes like this: "You must have the discipline to confront the most brutal facts of your current reality, whatever they might be."[xiii] While Collins was primarily talking about organizations in his book, these principles fit snugly into both our personal lives and our profession.

Start by truly understanding where we stand today. And that means embracing the whole package – the good, the bad, and even the downright ugly. Being brutally honest with yourself is the starting point, and let me tell you, people who aspire for excellence are masters at this. They stare their reality in the face, especially when it's uncomfortable.

Later in Good to Great, Fred Perdue of Pitney Bowes described looking at the brutal facts this way, "When you turn over rocks and look down at the squiggly things underneath, you can either put the rock down, or you can say, my job is to turn over rocks and look at the squiggly things even if what you see can scare the hell out of you."[xiv] Most people will look at the rock and put it right back, quickly. Why is that? Most people would rather not look at the ugliness that lies beneath. We, in policing, don't have that luxury of choosing to look, we absolutely must. Then we can either adjust or simply continue conducting business as usual and expecting different results.

Remember the infamous question Dr. Phil loves to ask? "How's that working out for you?" It's time for some serious introspection. Yes, I get it, peeking under rocks to discover squiggly things can be gross and unsettling. But here's the thing – that discomfort is the point. I want you to feel uneasy enough to examine your current situation.

That discomfort should be the push you need to navigate through the challenges our police force faces today. Use this emotion to create positive change in both policing and society. See, if you're comfortable where you are, then you won't have a reason to change. Why would you? Getting out of your comfort zone requires that you first decide that you are uncomfortable. People of excellence will look closely, as agonizing as it may be, because they understand that it must be done to remove the 'squiggly things' from our lives and in our case, our valued profession.

Remember to look at the squiggly things.

CHAPTER 12
PEOPLE STILL BELIEVE IN YOU

It's easy to feel like trust and respect for the police have taken a nosedive, especially considering the current climate. But let's take a moment to see the big picture. Believe it or not, despite the overall percentage is sloping downward, the police still rank among the highest when it comes to Americans' confidence in institutions. The police still rank higher than even the church, the news media, and not surprised, Congress.

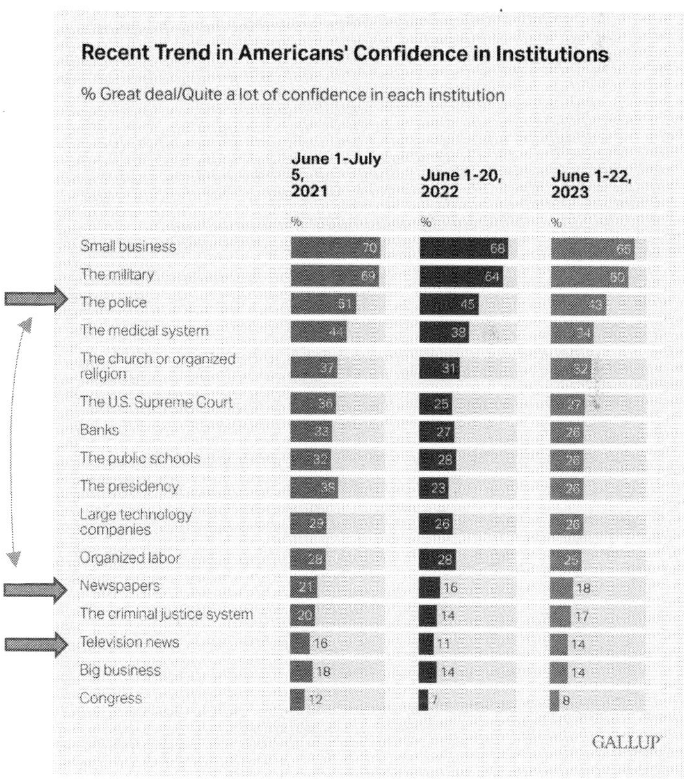

[xv]

Is there still work to be done? Not only yes, but hell yes! We have some work to do. Excellence does not allow complacency or mediocrity.

Ever wondered about how the public forms their opinions about the police? Or how much sway the media really holds over our profession? It's a debate worth diving into. The media, well, they seem to have a soft spot for negative stories involving the police, right? But here's the twist – do we really think people base their perceptions solely on media portrayals? Could it be that they form opinions from their personal interactions and experiences with officers like you? Food for thought. I believe they do. Ask yourself, what was your perception of police officers before becoming one?

What Media?

Speaking of the media, let's tackle the trust issue head-on. When officers voice their concerns about today's policing environment, their lack of trust in the media is often front and center. It's understandable; the media seems to have a knack for highlighting the negatives, overshadowing the countless positive aspects and stories in policing. But here's where things get interesting.

Year after year, the polls tell us a compelling story. The public puts way more faith in and trusts the police over the media. Again, look at where the media ranks on the same Gallup Poll listed institutions; a whopping 10 out of 16 for newspapers and 12 of 16 for television media. That's a powerful testament to the trust you've earned. Remember, when it comes to trust, the police still win every time.

Ever wonder why reporters scramble to interview a uniformed police officer or snag a departmental statement for their stories? It's simple – your presence adds credibility to their reports.

They see the polls too! And here's something to chew on – maybe you're giving the media a bit too much credit when it comes to shaping public opinion. That's not to say they're insignificant, but they might not wield as much influence as you believe they do.

Shift that energy back to what you can control – that's you, your actions, and the connections you make in your community. We can effectively control the narrative by the way we police- with fairness, dignity, and respect.

CHAPTER 13
EXCELLENCE IS IN THE DETAILS

"If you are going to achieve excellence in big things, you develop the habits in little matters. Excellence is not an exception; it is a prevailing attitude." General Colin Powell

If we truly grasp the concept that greatness thrives in the smallest details – echoing General Powell's words about the power of those "little matters," then we should take this wisdom and apply it to policing. I firmly believe that the key to our profession's success is by directing our attention towards the particulars, or details, of every interaction between law enforcement and citizens.

ID175156751 © Monkey Business Images Dreamstime.com

Picture this: several years ago, I decided to remodel my bathroom. And when I say remodel, I mean I gutted that thing down to the bare bones. Floors, walls, everything. Yes, I know, what was I thinking? Now, let me put it out there – I'm no Bob Vila. I've fixed minor stuff before, sure, but this was a whole new ballgame.

YouTube became my lifeline. I asked questions, invested in the right tools, and embarked on this grand DIY adventure.

ID30998883 © Ekays |Dreamstime.com

I realized how important the details were to go above being just being functional. The big stuff, like installing the vanity or putting in whole tiles, wasn't as tough as I'd anticipated. What drove me to the brink of madness? The teeny-tiny details. Think about it – precise paint lines, matching knobs, that flawless caulking, and those meticulous tile cuts. I can't even begin to count the trips between the bathroom and the wet saw for those darn precise cuts.

If I had skimped on the details, however, my bathroom might have been functional, but it wouldn't have been the masterpiece I was aiming for. And trust me, functional isn't what I had in mind. My aim was to build something to be proud of, something that screamed "excellence." Plus, I was the only one who truly understood how much sweat equity I'd poured into it. I owned it.

Let's add some wisdom gained from that bathroom ordeal and a few other projects along the way.

1. **Details Matter** – Obsessing over the details catapulted my project to excellence. Those details added value, making my home better than before.

2 **Functionality vs. Excellence** – They're not the same. Functionality is the baseline, the bare minimum. Sure, I could have stopped at functionality, but that's not what I wanted. Excellence, on the other hand, made me push past the ordinary.

3 **Right Tools** – having the right tools was a game-changer. My basic toolkit wasn't enough to go big. I had to invest in precise tools tailored for those exquisite details that my hammer and screwdriver couldn't handle.

Now, let's apply these nuggets to the world of policing:

1. **Details Matter** – Apply this concept to every police-citizen interaction. It's not just about marking off another call on the list; it's about diving into the details. For example, are you listening, truly listening? Are you being patient and empathetic, paying attention to the nuances of the situation? Are you solving the problem at hand? That is where excellence takes root.

2. **Functionality vs. Excellence** – Imagine you're just delivering a basic service – that's functionality. Now, imagine every encounter being an opportunity to make

a difference, to elevate the experience. That's excellence. It's about going above and beyond the call of duty, not because you must, but because you choose to. Huge difference.

ID62037859 © Oleg Dudko |Dreamstime.com

3. **Right Tools** – Just like I needed the right tools to transform my bathroom, you need the right tools to achieve excellence in policing It's not just about your physical gear; it's also about your mindset. Keep adding tools to your duty belt.

Empathy, communication, agility, de-escalation techniques are just some your tools needed for success. Remember, be like the cheetah and its agility. Don't just rely on one skill or tool, adapt, and select the best one for the situation at hand.

Here's the takeaway: the excellence we're striving for in policing isn't hidden in grand gestures; it's nestled in the details of each encounter. It's in the way you approach someone in distress, the way you communicate with respect, the way you navigate challenging situations with empathy. Remember, the little matters aren't little after all; they're the essence of excellence in policing.

CHAPTER 14
3 PHASE POLICE-CITIZEN ENCOUNTER MODEL

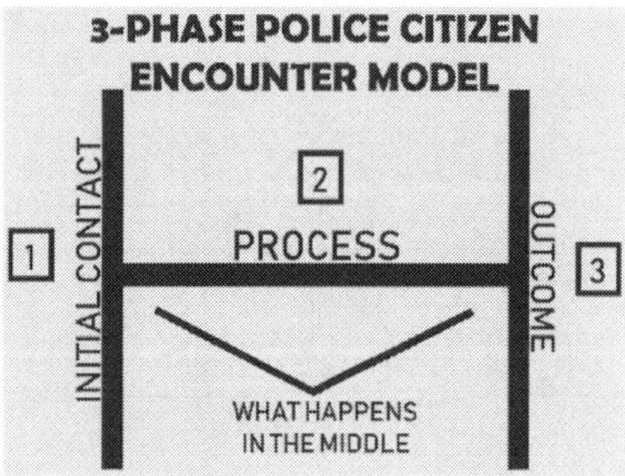

In this chapter, let's zoom in on the micro level of policing, delving into the intricate details. We'll break down police-citizen encounters into three distinct phases: the Initial Contact, the Process, and the Outcome. The intention behind this dissection is to provide you with a new perspective and a practical framework for grasping and applying the concepts discussed in this book. This book aims to shed light on how every police-citizen encounter might appear from a citizen's viewpoint.

The ultimate objective of this book is to equip you with a more profound understanding of how citizens perceive you and empower you to effectively navigate your interactions with the public, thus elevating their satisfaction and fostering a positive public opinion about their experiences with you.

During my Excellence in Policing seminars for both police officers of all ranks, I begin by posing this question: "Out of these three phases – the Initial Contact, the Process, and the

Outcome – which do you believe holds the most significance for citizens in terms of their satisfaction with police service?" Here's the thing – all three phases are important to citizens. No matter which phase you pick, you're right. however, for some of you, your choice will be a little more on the mark. But let's hold on to that thought for now.

Welcome to the ***Initial Contact*** phase – the very beginning of the police-citizen encounter. Picture this: you're out there, whether it's a traffic stop, responding to a 911 call, or even just walking into a Starbucks (my personal favorite). This phase encompasses not only the nature of the contact but also the citizen's perception of its legality. Remember, we're looking at this through the lens of a citizen's experience. This is where first impressions unfold, and believe it or not, both sides are sizing each other up just as you would when meeting someone new. Both parties might secretly wonder, "Who's this person? Are they going to be friendly or just another asshole? First impressions, it's a human thing – we all do it.

Here's the twist though: many citizens already have a preconception of you, the police officer, even before meeting you face to face. Unfair as it might be, it's reality. Let's be honest, (remember those squiggly things) – it's not hard for the police to start off on the wrong foot.

A poorly chosen word, a sarcastic remark (we'll dive into sarcasm later), or even silence – which by the way, can leave way too much room for confusion – may set things off on the wrong track. It's amazing how an officer's tone, body language, or mere presence can set a negative tone. Sound familiar? We all know officers like that. But hey, here's the silver lining –

there's hope! If things start off a bit rocky, fear not, because you have the next phase – the Process – to turn things around.

Now, let's dive into the second phase – the ***Process,*** or as I like to call it, what happens in the middle. This phase unfolds between the Initial Contact and the Outcome of the encounter. It's the space where the officer's decision-making process kicks into gear and citizens' opinions start to crystallize. This part is crucial for a bunch of reasons. Here's the twist: even if the officer's first interaction (Initial Contact) wasn't the greatest, there's still hope to shift the trajectory of the citizen's perception of you and how you treated them. How? Well, it's about being intentional and appropriately steering your actions in the right direction.

Now, hold onto your seats because we'll delve deeper into the concepts of managing perception and procedural justice later in the book – ideas that squarely fit into this phase. But for now, here's the gist: procedural justice revolves around the way authority figures treat people, and citizens care about this more than anything else. They want to feel that they treated with a sense of fundamental fairness, dignity, and respect. Keep this in mind: citizens will mostly judge whether they were treated fairly based on what you do during this Process. Your actions in this phase have a powerful influence in shaping their perception of their overall experience of you.

The final phase is the ***Outcome.*** This is the result of the police-citizen encounter or what you probably refer to as the disposition of the call. The Outcome can be anything from issuing a citation, making an arrest, or giving someone a warning, among other things. The Outcome will be viewed by the citizen as either favorable or unfavorable. This will depend on whether the citizen feels the violation (law) is legitimate *and* if the citizen perceives the officer's decision-making process was fundamentally fair. Tom Tyler is a well-known researcher who wrote, "*...people will be concerned with whether they receive fair outcomes, arrived at through a fair procedure, rather than with the favorability of the outcomes.*[xvi] In other words, *fairness* trumps even perceived favorable outcomes for citizens. These concepts of legitimacy and procedural justice are the result of Tom Tyler and Tracy Meares' research in these areas and will be expanded in the book.

Remember that question about which phase citizens consider most vital? The majority usually opt for either the Initial Contact or the Outcome. But, in reality, the heart of the matter for citizens is the Process, the middle part of the encounter. I must admit, I was a bit taken aback when I dug into the research. My own beliefs were shaken up. Interestingly, I initially assumed the Outcome was the front-runner.

Now, consider this: what if police officers operated under the assumption that the Outcome mattered most to citizens? It might lead officers to disregard how they treat citizens throughout the encounter, focusing solely on delivering a perceived favorable outcome. You might have heard an officer say, "Can you believe she complained? That's bullshit!" I gave her a warning! I should've issued her a ticket!" These officers could be outcome focused. Yet, it's clear how this approach could dent police efforts to build community trust and confidence. Such a mindset might hinder the police from exceeding citizens' expectations during these encounters.

Remember, people value a fair process more than the outcome. I should emphasize that nothing is absolute when dealing with human beings, so please keep that in mind as we move forward.

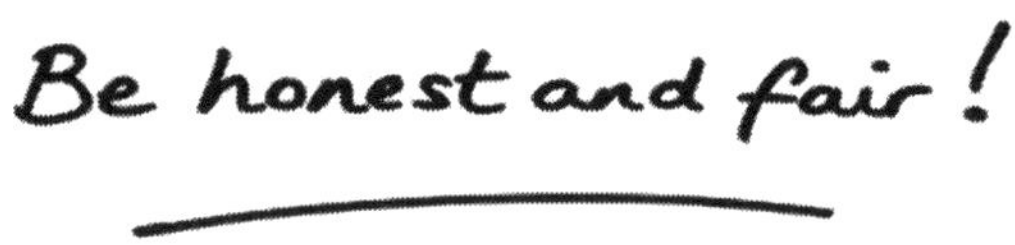

CHAPTER 15
JUST A TRAFFIC STOP?

ID13594631 © Firebrandphotography Dreamstime.com

Business owners know that understanding and catering to customers' needs and desires is paramount to success. And guess what? It's no different for us if we're aiming to surpass citizen expectations and thrive. Let's face it, we're in the service industry, whether we're fully embracing that term or not – which is why we're often referred to as "servants." But don't get this confused with weakness.

Now, have you ever pondered what citizens truly expect from you? It's a question worth considering. I can vividly recall one of the most eye-opening experiences I had during my time as the chief spokesperson for my department in a major television market. There was an incident that occurred during that period which left a lasting impression on me.

Our department was on the brink of releasing a dash cam video that had all the makings of a media frenzy. You see, this footage featured a mix of intense emotions, an NFL running back, and law enforcement – a recipe for quite the stir.

Surprisingly, the incident revolved around a simple traffic stop. It wasn't an instance of questionable officer-involved shooting or excessive use of force caught on tape. Nope, this was a 'routine' traffic stop. Yet, this seemingly ordinary traffic stop escalated into a national spectacle, igniting a fervent debate. You might recall seeing this incident on the news or hearing about it from others.

The story:

Late one night during a patrol shift, an officer noticed a car with its hazard lights blinking, breezing through a red light. Swiftly, the officer activated the flashing red and blue lights and tailed the vehicle into a hospital's emergency parking lot, ready to make a routine stop. But here's where things took an unexpected turn – the personal interaction that unfolded marked the heart of the encounter.

What the officer didn't know was that the driver was racing to the hospital with his wife to see their ailing mother-in-law, teetering on the edge of life. The wife, understandably emotional, rushed out of the car in a bid to reach her dying mother. Unaware of the circumstances, the officer insisted the driver remain seated, demanding the usual identification and insurance paperwork. The driver, in a rush and trying to explain their critical situation, found himself tangled in a web of paperwork demands.

The officer, seemingly more concerned about following protocol than empathizing with the emotional turmoil, persisted. Even when an ER nurse came out to convey the urgency of the situation and another officer arrived to intervene, the first officer didn't waver, in fact, he doubled down. Threats of towing the vehicle and even arrest were flung at the driver. Tragically, amidst this encounter, the driver's mother-in-law passed away.

Now, fast forward to when the dash cam video of this incident hit the media. Keep in mind, this all began as a 'straightforward' traffic stop. The news story, accompanied by the video footage, played out on the local evening news, sparking a fiery reaction. Overnight, my voicemail was inundated with angry messages from citizens. Citizens from all over the nation demanded answers and left messages like, "How dare you, officers treat anyone like that," and, "Who the hell do you think you all are?" Calls poured into the police media office and every patrol substation, echoing people's frustration.

In response, our department's leadership posted a statement on our website to address the escalating situation – a scenario entirely unheard of. The story's magnitude led to a press conference, led by Police Chief David Kunkle. Such a significant situation demanded the voice of the top cop and in a timely manner.

Chief Kunkle stepped up during the press conference the following morning, extending a sincere public apology to the family for the distressing experience they had with one of our officers. He candidly remarked, "His behavior, in my opinion, did not show the common sense, discretion, and compassion we expect from our officers." The Chief owned up to the lapse in judgment during the incident, emphasizing that it did not represent the department's values. Even though the national media kept the story alive for a few more days, the barrage of calls from citizens eventually dwindled and ceased. It was almost as if the community and nation collectively sighed in relief upon hearing the heartfelt message from the chief.

The Get-It Factor

In my view, the community resonated with what I like to call the Chief's "Get-It Factor." Citizens want to see that the police truly "get it" – that they truly understand their concerns and needs. It's vital for us, as police, to always remember that we are citizens first and foremost. Wearing the uniform doesn't separate us from the community; rather, it makes us more a part of it. This incident prompted me to contemplate what the community genuinely expects from the police and how we could transform this experience into a learning opportunity for all. True excellence demands nothing less.

Speaking as someone who appreciates visual thinking, I imagined Ms. Smith at her home, in Anytown, USA, watching the news story unfold. As she takes in the unfolding narrative, she begins processing what she's witnessing, attempting to comprehend it all. As the encounter unravels, gradually, a sense of unease creeps in, setting off an internal struggle. You see, Ms. Smith, like so many citizens, respects and supports the police, willing to give them the benefit of the doubt. On one hand, she's relieved that someone else is handling that late-night traffic stop, acknowledging the inherent danger of police work. Simultaneously, she recognizes the urgency of the family's situation.

Her internal struggle intensifies when the interaction between the officer and the driver kicks off. Just envision Ms. Smith closely observing both sides, attempting to piece together this unfolding scene before her eyes. Initially, she's inclined to trust that the officer knows what he's doing. However, as the signs of a legitimate family emergency become more apparent, her comprehension falters. At some point, during their interaction, Ms. Smith finds herself unable to support the officer any longer. In her perspective, the officer's actions have crossed a line this time.

What if this happened to me?

What happened to Ms. Smith? What was the moment that made her think, "Enough is enough?" Ms. Smith, like many others, placed herself in that same situation. She couldn't help but feel, "What if I were in a rush to see my mother one last time, only to be denied that chance? What if those were my own children trying to say goodbye to me in my final moments, and we missed that opportunity?" These were the thoughts echoing in the minds of countless viewers as they witnessed this encounter unfold. They inserted themselves into that same scenario and didn't like what they saw – and even more so, how they felt. The entrusted authority, the trust and consent given to that officer, had been grossly mishandled.

Let's dive a bit deeper. I don't possess insight into the officer's mindset that night; I can only gauge from his actions. I am aware, though, that there were no winners here. It's crucial to remember that this incident affected not only the lives of those involved, but also the officer's career and personal life. To my understanding, this was an officer who put in the hard work, consistently performing above average and often leading in his sector's activities. Yet, it took just one negative encounter to overshadow all of that. Fair or unfair, that's the reality of our chosen profession. Every single encounter carries weight.

CHAPTER 16
3 C'S OF COMMUNITY EXPECTATIONS

As I've traveled around the country sharing Excellence in Policing with officers, there's a recurring leadership challenge that stands out - the lack of engagement from first-line supervisors with their teams. Leaders, the question is this: Are you doing enough to shield your officers from crossing that metaphorical point of no return? Are you truly observing your officers in action? I'm not just talking about the "hot calls" like shootings and robberies; I mean the routine calls and traffic stops where there's significant personal interaction with citizens.

Are you paying attention to citizen complaints that might indicate a pattern of behavior that could harm your officers' careers and lives? In essence, do you genuinely care enough to take all these steps and more? I believe you do. Ensuring your officers are safeguarded physically and professionally is your primary duty.

Here's a simple method to convey community expectations to your officers, something I call the 3 C's of Community Expectations. While there are more factors, if officers keep these in mind when acting, they will be better protected, and citizen satisfaction increased. Another win-win.

COMPETENCE - Citizens anticipate the police to be proficient at their job, especially when it involves having the authority to restrict people's freedom. Fortunately, law enforcement does a commendable job of training officers in the essentials. While mistakes happen, officers are generally proficient. However, learning should never cease to guarantee that an officer's competence is never questioned.

In the traffic stop incident mentioned earlier, citizens didn't have qualms with the traffic stop itself; they deemed it legitimate. In contrast, not taking any initial action after observing the driver clearly running a red light, might have raised different concerns. Most citizens comprehend the safety concerns for officers during traffic stops. People understand that others might fabricate stories and, albeit infrequently, use desperate measures like pulling into an emergency room parking lot to dodge a ticket!

COMPASSION - Citizens don't want to interact with robots; they prefer dealing with genuine human beings! We all have emotions, and sometimes it's okay to express them. Remember the GET-IT Factor; compassion helps you acquire it. The police must never forget to place themselves in the citizen's situation to convey that they understand. I'm not advocating for hugs all around in every situation. You're not Oprah with the, "You get a hug, she gets a hug, everyone gets a hug!" I'm simply saying, be kind. Show people you care because you do. Be human.

COMMON SENSE - Yes, your Field Training Officer was right when she told you 90% of this job is common sense. Citizens truly appreciate it and respect you more when you use it. Let's start with the Merriam-Webster definition of common sense: the ability to think and act sensibly in a reasonable way and make sound decisions. Use your good judgment! Be agile (remember the cheetah), fair and reasonable.

While I'm not entirely certain if common sense can be taught, I've asked people to define it, and most find it challenging. People inherently understand what common sense looks like, even though it may be difficult to articulate. Here's my definition- "In policing, common sense is acknowledging that we all share this world and want the same things from it. It's making decisions that serve the greater good, including you *and* those you encounter." Always factor the totality of a situation, placing yourself in their shoes, and treat them as you'd want an officer to treat you or your loved ones under the same circumstances. Allow this to guide your approach in every police-citizen encounter.

D21332904© 72soul |Dreamstime.com

PRESCRIPTION: TAKE 2 EACH PRIOR TO EVERY SHIFT WITH OR WITHOUT YOUR FAVORITE ENERGY DRINK

PART IV

AUTHORITY, POWER AND LEGITIMACY

"Authority is a gift from those you serve.
How you use it is your gift back to them."

CHAPTER 17
AUTHORITY AND POWER

Authority comes from the people - an enduring truth that remains unchanged. Embarking on the path to excellence requires a profound understanding of the distinction between authority and power, particularly in the context of contemporary policing, which might be more pertinent than ever. Both hold importance, and it is the duty of law enforcement to meticulously gauge when and how to use each of them.

Authority is delegated influence, the granted right to govern.[xvii] For our purpose here, power, or force, conversely, signifies strength or the application of physical might to achieve an objective. Take a moment to contemplate the term 'delegated.' It signifies entrusting control, responsibility, and authority to someone, an act of designating another as their representative.[xviii]Authority, bestowed upon the police by the public, is something that should be treated with reverence. Ponder this: the community has vested their faith in you, trusting that you will act rightly and for honorable motives on *their* behalf. You stand as their representative.

Picture a scene: a uniformed police officer positioned in the middle of a street; palm raised towards oncoming traffic. The drivers, sensing the signs of authority, instinctively comply (most of the time) with the officer's direction. Here, the oncoming traffic possesses the physical power, yet it's the officer's authority that commands compliance. It's the authority that motivates the driver to stop.

Conversely, envision the same officer relying solely on physical power to stop the cars and trucks—well, the outcome is easy to predict. In this scenario, the drivers wield the power. This simple illustration underscores a vital distinction between authority and power. In the realm of policing, both elements hold essential roles in upholding societal order, addressing conflicts, and finding solutions within the community.

Employing power without the support of legitimate authority can be risky territory. Imagine the challenge of utilizing physical force, or power, without the public's recognition of your rightful authority—whether to defuse a situation or safeguard a life. Contemporary society is actively pushing for reduced use of force by the police—a development that benefits everyone, including law enforcement. Hence, it's paramount for officers to lean more towards leveraging their authority. Enhancing our influence (authority) can be achieved through the practice of procedural justice. This practice leads to heightened police credibility, resulting in bolstered legitimacy.

In the world of policing, authority and power are intertwined, not mutually exclusive. Yet, without trust first, authority crumbles. When authority falters, policing becomes considerably more hazardous. Next, we delve into the two facets of authority: legal and legitimate. Officers should never underestimate the value of their delegated authority. Think of authority in this light: Authority is a gift from those you serve. How you use it is your gift back to them.

CHAPTER 18
LEGITIMATE VS. LEGAL AUTHORITY

Legitimate Authority

In the realm of authority, there exist two types that warrant discussion. The first is legitimate authority, a form of influence that, much like respect, is earned over time. It's what amplifies your impact and command. Legitimacy and trust primarily hinge on citizens' perception that the police genuinely prioritize their welfare.[xix] But what does having citizens' "best interest in mind" truly entail? Let's examine the heart of the matter.

Officers, understandably, are trained to protect themselves (CYA) in every move they make. Again, what your field training officer told you is true, "Always cover your ass!" This practice is pivotal for securing your livelihoods and providing for your families—an essential aspect. However, the issue arises when officers exclusively act out of self-interest while making decisions and enforcing laws. This tendency can clash with the goal of fostering trust and legitimacy within the community.

The relationship between these "competing interests" can spark conflict when officers are solely focused on self-gain or career preservation. The crux is that the police should always operate in the best interest of both the community and the police force when making decisions and acting on them. The officer's choices should mirror the desires of their citizens (recall common sense). Do you wish to reside in a secure neighborhood? Do you anticipate that fellow officers would have your best interests at heart if you encountered them off-duty? Better yet, how would you expect another officer to act towards a loved one, mother, wife, daughter, son, on a traffic stop or if they called 911? I know you would want those officers to act with excellence.

The term "community" can be dissected into two words: "common" and "unity." Our shared attributes are the very bonds that unite us—creating the concept of community. Again, wearing a uniform doesn't separate you from the community; instead, it makes you more a part of it! At the beginning of the book, I included Sir Robert Peel's Nine Principles as a reminder of the police's original purpose. These principles remain relevant today. Pertaining to community, one principle stands out: "The police are the public and the public are the police." We are inseparable.

When confronted with decisions, a straightforward question to ask yourself is, "How will my actions impact the entire community?" In most cases, your actions will be beneficial for the community, whether it involves apprehending a drunk driver or issuing a citation for hazardous driving. Even something as minor as handing out a parking ticket can contribute to the greater good. Most individuals can comprehend and support your actions when they serve the common good. This creates trust.

However, it's when officers go out of their way to accumulate activity or engage in unnecessary actions solely to protect their self-interest. This may cause citizens to grow frustrated and begin questioning the true intentions of officers. This is the juncture where the conversation pivots to quality versus quantity. If your commitment is to nurturing trust, then it's crucial for officers to take actions guided by the right inspiration.

"The police should always act in the best interest of both the community and the police when making decisions and acting."

Legal Authority

The other part of authority is legal authority, which stems from the Constitution and state as well as local statutes.[xx] However, relying exclusively on legal authority can present a dilemma, as life seldom adheres to rigid rules or laws. This is where officers who perceive the world in black and white can find themselves entangled in complex situations. The intricacies of life necessitate the ability to navigate the gray areas effectively. Common sense and sound judgment must take precedence, guiding decisions that serve the best interests of both the police and the community.

The phrase "...life doesn't always fit into rules or laws" encapsulates this reality succinctly. While leaning solely on legal authority might yield short-term results, it is bound to be counterproductive in the long run. An "us against them" mindset or an approach that presumes "we know what's best for them" can erode public confidence and trust in police organizations. To avoid such a scenario, it's imperative for the police to gain a clearer understanding of the community's needs and expectations.

Professor Dennis Rosenbaum astutely observed that "residents will insist on aggressive policing and enforcement up to the point where it directly affects them, their family, or their friends, who frequently end up in jail or report being mistreated by police."[xxi] For instance, the application of zero-tolerance enforcement should be exercised judiciously; relying solely on legal authority in this context might inadvertently result in perceived mistreatment by the police.

Communities, especially those in high-crime areas (known as hot spots), should be able to experience both safety and freedom, without being forced to choose one over the other. Disregarding the community's perception of their police department would hinder the prospect of making a meaningful impact.

"…life doesn't always fit into rules or laws,
so don't force it."

Distinguishing between legitimate and legal authority is significant. Prioritizing and leveraging legitimate authority tends to yield a more voluntary compliance and cooperation from the public, fostering a willingness to grant the police the benefit of the doubt in various situations, including scandalous ones. In the era of social media, possessing the benefit of the doubt becomes a compelling advantage.

Gone are the days when a video took minutes to upload and circulate; platforms like Facebook Live bring events to the world in real time, reshaping the dynamics of information dissemination. The luxury of responding at a leisurely pace is a relic of the past for police leaders.

Imagine a scenario where residents instinctively extend the benefit of the doubt to their police department, even if momentarily, allowing the department to present accurate facts and respond effectively before making their own judgment. Achieving such a scenario necessitates an elevated level of trust between the community and law enforcement. In this rapidly evolving world, cultivating legitimate authority that garners public confidence is essential, creating a foundation for transparent and informed interactions between the police and the communities they serve.

CHAPTER 19
TRUST AND LEGITIMACY

In the pursuit of excellence, staying abreast of the latest literature in our field is essential. In May 2015, the Final Report of the President's Task Force on 21st Century Policing emerged as a significant milestone. This report serves as a roadmap not just for surviving the challenges confronting law enforcement today, but for thriving amidst adversity. I strongly recommend delving into the report's entirety, available here:

https://cops.usdoj.gov/pdf/taskforce/TaskForce_FinalReport.pdf

As leaders, we must consistently challenge our belief systems. To achieve this, we must immerse ourselves in academic discourse, engaging critically with issues shaping our profession.

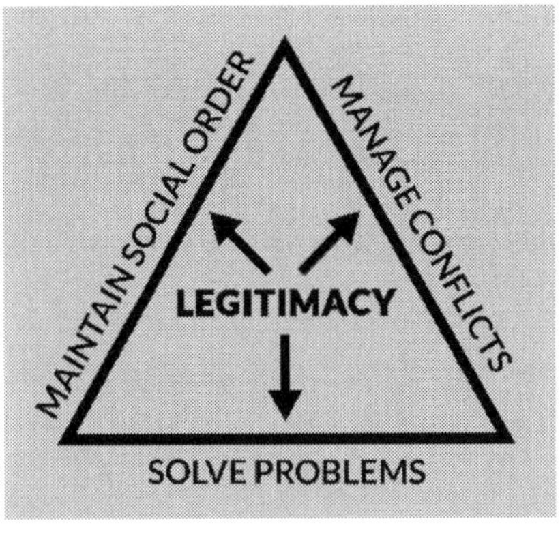

The first cornerstone of 21st Century Policing is Building Trust and Legitimacy. This foundational concept underscores the significance of police legitimacy in establishing and sustaining community trust. Police legitimacy embodies the notion that law enforcement should wield authority to preserve order, manage conflicts, and address community issues. Ponder this for a moment: "the police ought to be allowed to exercise their authority..." When your community perceives you as legitimate, they not only expect you to wield your authority but cheer you on in doing so!

"When your community perceives you as legitimate, they not only expect you to wield your authority but cheer you on in doing so!"

The power of legitimacy is immense; police must work tirelessly to nurture and amplify it. Increased legitimacy grants more authority, a reflection of delegated influence. Leadership and influence are inseparable, evident in individuals with followers willing to charge into adversity. Apply this to policing, and exceeding community expectations becomes more seamless. Citizens yearn for your success; they understand that in your triumph, the community thrives. Everyone wins.

Social Deposits

Building trust is more than just making appearances at community gatherings or addressing neighborhood watches, although these efforts hold significance. Trust isn't exclusively nurtured by such activities; it arises largely from how the public perceives their treatment by law enforcement. Continuously replenishing the trust account is imperative. Waiting for a crisis is too late. Every officer should be consistently making trust deposits in every interaction with citizens. Keep in mind, each police-citizen encounter is a testimonial for your department.

Our triumphs are measured by the degree of confidence and trust bestowed upon us by our citizens.

Why People Obey the Law

Let's ponder another question. Have you ever contemplated why most people abide by the law and how this alignment helps us? A substantial number adhere to the law due to the perception that those enforcing it possess the right to dictate behavior.[xxii] While punitive consequences serve as deterrents, relying solely on them falls short in impacting crime. Fortunately, the core of most individuals' obedience lies in their intrinsic values guiding them toward righteous actions. Though not infallible, these citizens, guided by their values, greatly assist the police in combating crime. Thus, the quest to build legitimacy directly bolsters our efforts.

Crime fighting is an inherent aspect of police work that remains essential. However, it's crucial to recognize that police officers can't tackle crime alone and achieve lasting success. This duty should always be a joint effort with the citizenry. Trust and confidence in the police are vital for establishing genuine partnerships in crime prevention. Without this trust, collaboration becomes challenging or even unattainable. The repercussions of lacking trust are significant, ranging from legal consequences like lawsuits to a reduced willingness among citizens to follow the law. In a nutshell, it's essential for the police to maintain legitimacy in the eyes of the community to effectively combat crime.

Consider how difficult your job as a cop would be if the people did not view you as a legitimate authority figure. It would not only be difficult, but also unsustainable. The police work would become more dangerous. Thus, fostering and enhancing police legitimacy is more than a desire; it is critical to our success. The more legitimate the police are regarded to be, the more powerful and secure our communities will be. As a result, pursuing excellence in policing is inextricably linked to the empowerment of legitimate authority.

CHAPTER 20
BUILDING LEGITIMACY WITH PROCEDURAL JUSTICE

Now that we've explored the significance of police legitimacy and its relevance to law enforcement, let's delve into strategies for enhancing it. One key approach to achieving legitimacy is by practicing procedural justice in every interaction between police officers and citizens. The concept of procedural justice has gained prominence in recent years, with researchers like Tom Tyler and Tracy Meares shedding light on its importance for our profession. Staying informed and engaged with their work is crucial to maintaining excellence in policing.

In the context of the 3-phase model (Initial Contact, Process, Outcome), this chapter focuses on the Process phase. People are often more concerned with the process they experience during police-citizen encounters, even more than the eventual outcome. Procedural justice entails treating citizens fairly, with dignity and respect, throughout these encounters. When citizens perceive that they are treated fairly and respectfully, their attitudes towards the police become more positive, leading to higher levels of trust and confidence.

This, in turn, elevates police legitimacy. Positive attitudes drop when citizens feel they were treated unfairly or with disrespect by the police, resulting in decreased trust and legitimacy.[xxiii] Therefore, procedural justice should boost every police-citizen interaction, as it fosters legitimacy.

While crime fighting remains a central aspect of policing, effective crime reduction requires partnership between police officers and the community. Solely relying on law enforcement to combat crime is not sustainable in the long run. Building trust and confidence in the police is essential for establishing true collaboration in crime prevention.

Without these foundational elements, the effectiveness of joint efforts to combat crime is compromised. The consequences of lacking trust and legitimacy are significant, ranging from legal challenges to a decline in public willingness to comply with the law.[xxiv] Therefore, police legitimacy is a non-negotiable factor in effective crime fighting, and it's imperative for law enforcement to prioritize building and maintaining legitimacy in the eyes of the citizens they serve.

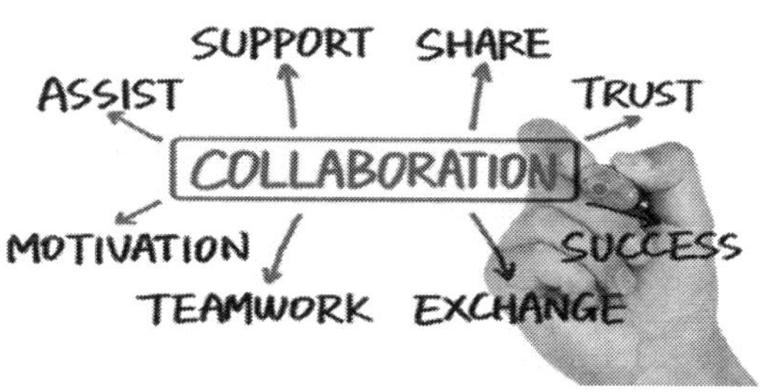

ID57433121 © Cacaroot |Dreamstime.com

CHAPTER 21
THE FOUR TENETS OF PROCEDURAL JUSTICE

1st Part- Decision Making

Voice: Tom Tyler's breakdown of procedural justice consists of two parts and four essential principles, all of which should be consistently applied during every encounter, particularly in the Process phase where people's majority of focus lies. The first part involves how an officer makes decisions. The first tenet, Voice, now comes into play.

This principle encompasses both listening to the citizen's perspective and explaining the officer's actions. By practicing these tenets, you can manage perception more effectively. Allowing citizens to share their side, even if it doesn't align with your decision, demonstrates a commitment to fairness and involvement. Furthermore, explaining your actions and rationale fosters openness and respect, enhancing the sense of procedural justice.

Neutrality: The second tenet according to Tyler, emphasizes the appearance of officer neutrality and impartiality. The concept of managing perception is pivotal here as well. While many officers operate with the right intentions, failing to manage perception can lead to misunderstandings or perceptions of bias. This can ultimately result in complaints, triggering a chain of events with potential consequences.

In a world where citizens are better informed and vigilant about police actions, managing perception becomes a critical power move. The responsibility falls on the police to proactively shape how they are perceived by the public, leveraging increased citizen awareness to foster trust and legitimacy.

"Police must play chess and not checkers;

managing perception will always be a power move."

Photo 1896987 | Chess © Hans Mageissen | Dreamstime.com

Story: A Lesson in Perception Management

Here's a story that paints a picture of why managing perception on patrol is a big deal.

There are these two patrol officers, right? They get a call about a suspicious person in a neighborhood. You know, the whole black shirt, jean shorts, and backpack kind of a deal. The neighborhood's been hit by vehicle burglaries lately, so people are on edge. Finally, this resident decides to dial 911 and spill the beans about the "sketchy" dude.

So, she steps outside to talk to the officers, gives them the lowdown about where the guy went – eastbound on her street. The officers just nod and say "thanks," then bust a U-turn and go the other way – westbound. She's probably thinking, "Seriously? Did they even hear me?"

But here's the kicker: the cops had a hunch that this guy, let's call him Johnny, hangs out at the C Store down the road to the west. That's why they flipped around. But guess what? They didn't bother explaining that to her, and she's left feeling like she wasted her time, and the police don't care.

This is where managing perception comes into play. If those officers had taken a few extra seconds to say, "Hey, we're pretty sure we know where this Johnny guy's hanging out, so we're headed that way," the resident would've been like, "Great, thanks for the heads up," and felt empowered rather than minimized. Instead, she's pissed and probably not too eager to call 911 again. See, a quick explanation can make all the difference between someone feeling respected and someone feeling brushed off. Managing perception is the secret sauce to keeping the community's trust intact.

2nd Part- Treatment

Respect: In the second part of procedural justice, the focus shifts to the way individuals are treated throughout the interaction. Here, the pivotal principle is "respect." It encapsulates the notion of valuing and honoring individuals due to their inherent worth.[xxv] This principle is universally desired by every citizen and underscores the essence of humane interaction.

Breaking it down into actionable steps, one of the foundation stones is active listening – genuinely engaging with what the individual is saying. Employing eye contact conveys undivided attention, enhancing the perception of being heard. Incorporating personalized understanding, like acknowledging shared experiences, contributes to the sense of respect. Furthermore, offering assistance and gratitude, when appropriate, strengthens this sentiment. These seemingly simple gestures collectively foster an environment of respect and fairness, augmenting positive interactions and fostering community trust.

Trustworthiness: Now, shifting our focus to the fourth principle of procedural justice – trustworthiness. This tenet centers on cultivating an image of reliability and transparency. It revolves around openly explaining your actions and the rationale behind them. By exhibiting transparency, you avoid appearing secretive or evasive, fortifying trust. Even nonverbal cues, such as facial expressions, play a role; studies suggest that a slightly happier countenance resonates with trustworthiness.[xxvi] Striking a balance between professionalism and approachability further enhances this perception, engendering trust.

In summary, procedural justice encompasses these four tenets: Voice, Neutrality, Respect, and Trustworthiness. Mastering these principles will significantly enhance the quality of police-citizen encounters. Studies suggest these results include the following: greater public deference to the police when the police have personal interactions with members of the community, increased compliance with the law, higher levels of cooperation with police efforts to manage crime, and stronger institutional support for police departments.[xxvii]

By treating individuals fairly, actively managing perceptions, and fostering transparency, law enforcement professionals contribute to building trust, legitimacy, and positive community relations. It's not just about enforcing laws; it's about establishing meaningful connections that uphold justice and create safer, more cohesive communities.

CHAPTER 22
PROCEDURAL JUSTICE IS GOOD FOR YOU

Let's talk safety – always a top priority for officers. And guess what? Practicing procedural justice is like a safety net. Here's the deal: when you treat people right and show them respect, they're more likely to go along with what you're asking. When people see you as someone with authority they can trust, you won't have to flex as much. And you know what that means? Less need for force or power, which directly lowers the risk of you unnecessarily becoming injured.

Consider this – when things get physical, injuries happen. You've more than likely have experienced it – been maced by your partner, suffered broken fingers, sprained this or that. It's not fun. But practicing procedural justice can help cut down on those situations to begin with. And, staying injury-free isn't just about you; it's about being there for your family and your team. Who can argue against being safe and sound? It's a win-win.

Practicing procedural justice can lower your stress at work. Stress automatically comes from just being a police officer. A Forbes article ranked police officers as the fourth most stressful job in 2016. And here's a startling fact: officers tend to live around 66 years, about a whole decade less than the average American male.[xxviii] That alone should be a wake-up call to bring down stress.

Now, let's hit on one of the most stressful parts of the job – dealing with citizen complaints, even when you know you've done nothing wrong. By the way, rudeness is the number one complaint in every department. You know how it goes – a citizen calls in, griping about you, and suddenly your sergeant is on the radio, telling you to head over to the station. Your mind races back through your day, wondering if you stepped on anyone's toes. "I guess I piss off," you wonder. And then, boom – your heart rate spikes, and your blood pressure follows suit as you drive to the station. There's something about hearing your sergeant or supervisor wants to chat that amp up your stress level.

A citizen complaint is usually over something such as not allowing the citizen to share their side, using a harsh or firm tone, or leaving the citizen feeling unfairly treated. These are all situations that procedural justice can help avoid in every single encounter. If practicing procedural justice helps you be healthier and live longer, than it's worth doing.

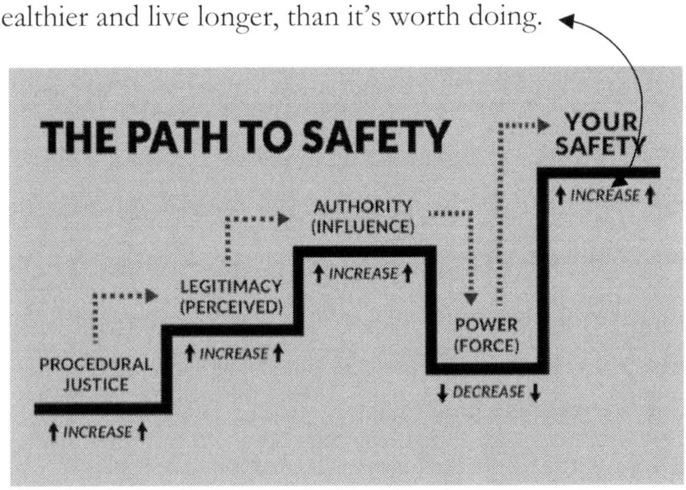

CHAPTER 23
PROMOTE MUTUAL RESPECT AND UNDERSTANDING

A significant challenge for both police officers and citizens is enhancing mutual respect and understanding between them. This is a must for successful policing today. One effective approach is practicing procedural justice in every interaction between police and citizens. The age-old saying about giving respect to earn respect holds true. If officers expect citizens to treat them with respect, they must initiate it. It's not a matter of disrespecting anyone, but rather, someone needs to take the lead as the responsible party, the adult in the room. That of course, is YOU. The community looks to you to assume that role.

"Every encounter is an opportunity to increase mutual understanding."

One of the conflicts officers must deal with often is citizens' belief that they fully comprehend an officer's job. As you've experienced, the reality is quite different – they usually don't. Remember one of the tenets of procedural justice is the importance of explaining an officer's actions and, crucially, the reasons behind those actions. When an officer takes the time to provide explanations, citizens can better grasp the circumstances and accept the outcomes. Furthermore, this enhances their comprehension of your role. Every encounter is an opportunity to increase mutual understanding. This practice also helps minimize complaints from citizens – another win-win situation.

Seek First to Understand

The "seek first to understand" guideline from Stephen Covey's 7 Habits of Highly Successful People is a good approach for police departments to implement. It highlights the significance of attentively listening and empathizing with others before acting. This notion is especially important in the context of policing when it comes to regulating public perceptions and sustaining community trust.

For police officers, applying the "seek first to understand" approach can be a valuable strategy. Officers that truly listen to community people, understand their issues, and empathize with their points of view promote a sense of validation and respect. Active listening not only aids in the development of strong connections, but it also allows officers to address situations more efficiently. Furthermore, by attempting to understand the needs and concerns of the community, police departments can modify their plans and activities accordingly. This method guarantees that law enforcement actions are aligned with community priorities, resulting in more meaningful and impactful outcomes.

Additionally, accepting this idea can assist law enforcement agencies in avoiding errors that may erode trust. Officers can avoid potential confrontations and miscommunications from growing by proactively correcting misunderstandings or misconceptions. The application of "seek first to understand" in police is essentially about promoting empathy, effective communication, and community-centered problem-solving. It recognizes the importance of understanding as a bridge between law enforcement and the community, ultimately leading to better relations, more trust, and increased public safety.

When Worlds Collide

It's a recurring scenario – the worlds of police and citizens collide. Again, the key challenge here is that many citizens believe they know the ins and outs of a police officer's job. You might have heard this referred to as the CSI effect, but these beliefs often contrast with the actual realities of policing.

An example of this disconnect gained national attention in an incident involving a veteran Cambridge Police Department Sergeant and a Harvard Professor in Cambridge, Massachusetts. Some of you may remember when this incident even led to a beer summit at the White House, hosted by President Obama, in an attempt to bridge the two worlds.

The incident's significance is that it could have transpired in Any Town, USA. While it achieved national notoriety, similar encounters between police officers and citizens play out daily at various levels. Commissioner Robert C. Haas of the Cambridge Police deserves credit for allowing scrutiny of this incident, as do Sgt. Crowley and Professor Gates for sharing their experiences to benefit policing. It's vital to note that this chapter aims not to criticize either party, but rather to draw lessons from this teachable moment.

In this chapter, our focus turns to the differing accounts of the incident, highlighting how enhancing mutual respect and understanding can effectively manage police-citizen encounters. You'll be surprised by the varying perspectives of Sgt. Crowley and Professor Gates on the same incident. Both versions are directly drawn from the Cambridge Review Committee's (CRC) final report, "Missed Opportunities, Shared Responsibilities: Final Report of the Cambridge Review Committee." I shared this case study in my first book, Excellence in Policing, and it is too good not to include it here again for you. For the purposes of this chapter and lesson, let's focus primarily on the interaction between the two parties as they describe entirely two different worlds. I strongly encourage you to read the entire case study titled *Missed Opportunities, Shared Responsibilities: Final Report of the Cambridge Review Committee* at:

http://www2.cambridgema.gov/CityOfCambridge_Content/documents/Cambridge%20Review_FINAL.pdf

The 911 Call

On July 16th, 2009, The Cambridge Emergency Communications Center (ECC), the city's 911 center, received a call at 12:43 p.m. According to the caller, an elderly woman had observed two men with suitcases attempting to enter a residence on Ware Street in Cambridge. The elderly woman expressed concern to the caller that the men were attempting to break into someone's home. The caller observed that the front door screen had been broken but expressed uncertainty about whether the men perhaps lived there and "just had a hard time with a key." At 12:46 p.m., a Cambridge Police patrol unit in the area was dispatched to respond to Ware Street for a "possible breaking and entering in progress."

According to Sergeant Crowley

Sergeant Crowley has a reputation for being a no-nonsense, by-the-book police officer. He has been commended for dedication and professional conduct for helping a diabetic victim avert a tragedy and for diligence that resulted in an arrest and successful investigative case closure. Among his peers, regardless of their race, Crowley is well liked and respected on the force. In 1993, Crowley was a campus police officer at Brandeis University when he administered CPR trying to save the life of former Boston Celtics player Reggie Lewis. He was selected by former Police Commissioner Ronnie Watson to teach a class on preventing racial profiling at the Police Academy in Lowell, Mass. He has conducted that training, along with an African American officer, for five years.

During the past five years, Sergeant Crowley has made twelve arrests, including one arrest of a disorderly person, one for disturbing the peace, and three for unlawful assembly. It is important to understand that sergeants, with multiple and varied supervisory and administrative duties, including guiding officers in arrest situations, do not normally make large numbers of arrests themselves.

Sergeant Crowley reported that he arrived at the Ware Street residence in full uniform, with his nametag and badge number clearly displayed, as required by the Police Department. The recording of the 911 call shows that the caller said she was "not really sure" about the race of the men attempting to enter the residence, but that "one looked kind of Hispanic."

But according to Crowley's Incident Report, by the time he arrived and spoke to the 911 caller on the sidewalk in front of the house, she told him that she had observed "what appeared to be two black males" on the porch. Crowley stated that the caller said she was suspicious because she saw one of the men wedging his shoulder into the door, as if he were trying to force entry.

In his Incident Report, Crowley reported that "since I was the only police officer on location and had my back to the front door," he asked the caller to wait for other responding officers while he investigated further. Crowley reported to the Committee that he walked onto Professor Gates' front porch and felt very exposed because of the large windows he had to pass by. He looked inside the home and saw an older black man in the foyer, whom Crowley, motioning with his hand, asked to step out onto the porch.

According to Crowley, the man, who later identified himself as Henry Louis Gates, Jr., refused, saying, "No, I will not." Crowley claimed that Gates demanded to know who Crowley was, and Crowley said he identified himself as "Sergeant Crowley from the Cambridge Police" and informed Gates that he was there to investigate a report of a break-in in progress at the residence. Crowley reports that it was at this point that Gates opened his door and exclaimed, "Why, because I am a black man in America?" Crowley stated that he then asked Gates if there was anyone else in the house, to which Gates yelled that it was none of his business. Crowley said that Professor Gates then accused Crowley of being a racist police officer.

Crowley said he assured Gates that he was responding to a citizen's call to the Cambridge Police Department and the caller was still present, outside. Crowley said Gates then telephoned an unknown person and asked that person to "get the chief," and then told whoever was on the line that he was dealing with a racist police officer. According to Crowley, Gates then told Crowley he had no idea who he was "messing" with and that he hadn't heard the last of this.

At this point in his Incident Report account, Crowley wrote, "While I was led to believe that Gates was lawfully in the residence, I was quite surprised and confused with the behavior he exhibited toward me." Crowley said he then asked Gates for photo identification so he could verify that Gates, in fact, resided there. Crowley said Gates refused initially but later complied, showing a Harvard identification card. Crowley reported that upon learning that Gates was affiliated with Harvard, he radioed ECC and requested the presence of the Harvard University Police, and then prepared to leave the premises.

Crowley reported that Gates again demanded to know Crowley's name, accused Crowley of being a racist police officer, and said that he, Gates, "wasn't someone to mess with." Crowley became aware that Officer Carlos Figueroa was present. Crowley said that Gates continued to request his name and badge number. Crowley said that he told Gates that he had already provided his name twice upon Gates' request, that he was leaving Gates' residence, and that if he had any other questions, he "would speak to him outside of the residence." Crowley said that "my reason for wanting to leave the residence was that Gates was yelling very loud and the acoustics of the kitchen and foyer were making it difficult for me to transmit pertinent information to ECC or other responding units."

According to Crowley, he walked outside and noticed "several Cambridge and Harvard University police officers assembled on the sidewalk," as well as the 911 caller and at least seven passers-by looking in the direction of Gates, who had followed Crowley outside. Crowley's account in his police report stated that Gates was continuing to yell and behave in a "tumultuous" manner. Crowley stated that he warned Gates that he was becoming disorderly, but that Gates ignored his warning and continued yelling, which caused the bystanders to appear "surprised and alarmed." Crowley said he warned Gates a second time while taking out his handcuffs, but that Gates again ignored his warning. Crowley then placed Gates under arrest.

Crowley reported that Gates objected to being handcuffed behind his back, because he said he was disabled and could not walk without a cane. Crowley ordered another officer to handcuff Gates with his hands in front and went into the house to retrieve Gates' cane. Crowley reported asking Gates if he wanted the property secured, to which Gates replied that the lock on the door was broken from a previous break-in attempt. A Harvard University maintenance person then arrived to secure the house.

Crowley's Incident Report states that Gates was arrested for disorderly conduct because he exhibited "loud and tumultuous behavior, in a public place, directed at a uniformed police officer who was present investigating a report of a crime in progress." Five days later, the Middlesex County District Attorney's Office dropped the charge against Gates. The City of Cambridge, the Cambridge Police Department, and Professor Gates released a joint statement saying that "the incident of July 16th, 2009, was regrettable and unfortunate," and that dropping the charge was "a just resolution to an unfortunate set of circumstances."

According to Professor Gates

Professor Gates is an American literary critic, educator, scholar, and writer. Professor Gates earned his M.A. and Ph.D. in English literature from Clare College at the University of Cambridge and his B.A. in history from Yale University, where he was a Scholar of the House. Professor Gates is currently the Alphonse Fletcher University Professor at Harvard University, where he is Director of the W.E.B. Du Bois Institute for African and African American Research. Gates has previously taught at Yale, Cornell, and Duke Universities.

Among his many other notable accomplishments, Gates was listed in Time as one of 1997's "25 Most Influential Americans." In January 2008, Gates co-founded The Root, a website dedicated to African American perspectives, published by The Washington Post Company. Gates also serves on the boards of many institutions, including the New York Public Library, the Aspen Institute, the Brookings Institution, the NAACP Legal Defense Fund, the Harlem Educational Activities Fund, and the Center for Advanced Study in the Behavioral Sciences located in Stanford, California.

According to published reports and Professor Gates' interview with the Cambridge Review Committee, he was arriving home from the airport on July 16th, 2009. A local limousine company dropped Gates off at his home. Gates attempted to enter through the front door of the property but had trouble because the door was damaged. Specifically, Gates reported seeing damage suggesting that someone had tried to jimmy the lock; he also noticed a large footprint on the door. The limousine driver, whom Gates referred to as Driss, assisted Gates in attempting to gain entry to the house. Gates ultimately entered the rear entrance with his key and attempted to open the front door from the inside.

Gates was able, with the driver's help, to force the front door open and proceed through with his luggage. The driver said that he noticed an elderly female looking at them from next door as they were trying to enter the house. Gates recalled Driss' comment at the time that the woman "was calling the police on us." Gates reported that he called the Harvard Real Estate office to report the damage; while he was on the phone, he noticed a uniformed police officer on his front porch. Gates opened the door, and the officer asked Gates to step outside. Gates said that the officer's tone of voice made the hairs on the back of his neck stand up, and he refused to step outside.

Gates said he told the officer that he lived there and was a faculty member at Harvard University, and that the officer then asked him for proof that he lived there. Gates said he went into his kitchen, followed by Crowley, to get his wallet, and then placed his open wallet showing his Harvard identification card and Massachusetts driver's license on the counter for Crowley to see. Gates said that Officer Crowley did not respond.

Gates said he asked for the officer's name and badge number on several occasions, but that the officer never responded or asked him if he was all right. Gates said that "the silence was deafening." Gates said he then said to the officer,

"You're not responding because I am a black man and you're a white officer."

Gates said that Crowley said, "We are done here," and turned to leave the house. Gates followed Crowley toward the front door, where he saw other police officers outside. When the officer left his home, Gates followed, still trying to get Crowley's badge number and name. Gates reported that as he again asked for the officer's identification, pointing his finger at Crowley's chest, the officer responded, "Thank you for accommodating my earlier request; now you're under arrest," and arrested him. Gates was then transported to the Cambridge Police Station and was held for four hours.

Gates told the Cambridge Review Committee that in retrospect, he would not have done anything differently, other than stepping outside onto the front porch after the encounter with Crowley inside the house. Gates said he could not understand why Crowley did not further explain why he had come to the house, but rather had remained silent. He said that during his encounter with Crowley, he became concerned that he was considered a suspect, because Crowley was not responding to his questions and seemed to take a long time studying his identification cards. He said he could not understand how Sergeant Crowley could think he was a burglar—a slight, elderly man who walks with a cane and who comes to the front door, telephone in hand, to talk to the police. "What criminal would do that?" he wondered.

This Was Avoidable

This incident was avoidable.[xxix] The Cambridge Review Committee (CRC) found that both Sgt. Crowley and Professor

Gates missed opportunities to deescalate the situation. The committee focused on misunderstandings, failed communications, and fear between the two men. While Sgt. Crowley was right about being cautious of a potentially dangerous encounter, once the threat was diminished, he should have taken steps to deescalate the situation.

On the other hand, Professor Gates should have complied with Sgt. Crowley's demands and should have tried to understand the situation from a police officer's point of view. A measure of respect may have helped deescalate the circumstances. Sgt. Crowley felt he "had no choice" but to arrest the professor. However, the CRC believed there could have been a better outcome. Perhaps Sgt. Crowley should have taken "greater pains" to explain the uncertainty and potential dangers of the call; additionally, his duty to assess the risks may have caused him to "adopt a seemingly abrupt tone."[xxx]

The CRC made it clear that the arrest of Professor Gates is not being questioned and noted that it was not unjustified. The point they did raise, however, is whether some police actions that may be "within policy" are not necessarily the best outcomes to a situation and may undermine the relationship between the police and the communities they serve.[xxxi]

Two Worlds

Same incident but viewed from two completely different worlds. Both parties were firmly convinced that their actions were justified. When they shared their perspectives with the Cambridge Review Committee, they both acknowledged being puzzled by each other's behavior. Sgt. Crowley and Professor

Gates never made an earnest attempt to understand each other's point of view.

Sgt. Crowley's primary concern was safety, with a hint of nabbing a potential burglar. However, Professor Gates felt like a suspect rather than a law-abiding citizen. Crowley's refusal to provide his name and badge number seemed like an abuse of power and an insult to Gates. This encounter's potentially risky nature underscores the importance of practicing procedural justice <u>once the threat subsides</u>. Explaining your actions afterward can be just as impactful as doing so during the heat of the moment (remember the Process).

Crowley did mention that he did try to offer his information to Gates, but Gates' yelling made it impossible to communicate effectively. Crowley interpreted Gates' repeated questions as hostility. Clearly, neither party endeavored to understand the other's perspective, leaving their worlds isolated. Remember, just because something is legally within your authority, doesn't mean it's always the best choice. And to the best of my knowledge, there's no law against "P.O.P" (pissed off the police) in any penal code – I've thoroughly checked. We all get it – there are individuals who need to be taken into custody. There's no denying that we encounter assholes out there. Most people, though, wouldn't swap places with you for any amount of money. Dealing with such situations isn't something they're eager to do.

Nonetheless, the police need to rise above that. Arresting someone to vent frustration or annoyance can land you in hot water and jeopardize your career. Moreover, these types of arrests contradict the very foundation of our efforts – building trust, mutual respect, and understanding. Navigating through this is like a game of chess, where discretion is our most valuable move. If you're the only one truly harmed, excluding physical harm, then finding solutions that don't involve arrest might be your best bet. Policing smarter is the name of the game today.

CHAPTER 24
DISCRETION

When engaging in any encounter, it's essential to ask yourself, "What outcome do I want?" or "What's the win?" This necessitates the ability to anticipate and plan 2 or 3 steps ahead, like chess, in order to enhance the quality of decisions made in the present moment. If it doesn't feel right, your decision probably isn't the best option.

However, the tool of discretion, which grants us the freedom to decide to act, is a double-edged sword. On one hand, it offers the capacity to tailor our actions to fit the unique circumstances at hand. On the other hand, it places a weighty responsibility on us to exercise it judiciously. Our choices have the potential to trigger significant outcomes, either positively or negatively, affecting both individuals and entire communities. Thus, wielding this power requires careful thought and good judgment.

Recognizing its significance, the United States Supreme Court has recognized the necessity of discretion for effective policing. Since the Terry decision in 1969, the Court has recognized that discretion is a central part of police methods. Courts have repeatedly ruled that police officers have both training and experience not common to others, based on which they should use increasingly wide discretion.[xxxii] This acknowledgment is a valuable tool for us. Yet, we must be proactive in safeguarding this capability by using it judiciously. Abusing discretion through unnecessary or abusive actions could jeopardize its legitimacy, hindering our ability to fulfill our duties effectively. Discretion is our greatest tool and our greatest liability. Use it wisely.

PART V

KNOW THYSELF AND EMBRACE OUR HUMANITY

"…grace has a place in policing."

CHAPTER 25
SELF-AWARENESS

In the realm of policing, where the stakes are high, the significance of self-awareness cannot be overstated. Just as situational leaders adapt their approaches to suit the situation, police officers must possess a high level of self-awareness to thrive in their demanding roles. Policing attracts a diverse array of individuals, but regardless of their backgrounds, cultivating emotional intelligence and self-awareness is indispensable for success in law enforcement.

The journey of self-awareness necessitates officers to dig deeply into their inner self. This encompasses analyzing thoughts, emotions, and behavior, thereby grasping their reactions to varying situations and interpersonal dynamics. Self-assessment tools tailored for emotional intelligence offer insights into strengths, weaknesses, and opportunities for personal growth.

Advantages of Self-Awareness in Policing

Officers who are self-aware are better able to interact with others. Recognizing one's own talents and limitations allows for effective handling of high-stress situations, building trust among communities, and making sound judgments under pressure. Furthermore, emotional awareness allows officers to understand the implications of their actions, creating positive relationships and neutralizing possible conflicts.

Emotional intelligence, integral to self-awareness, encapsulates recognizing and managing one's emotions, while empathizing with others. Officers possessing emotional intelligence exhibit self-confidence, empathy, and exceptional interpersonal skills. These attributes facilitate navigating the intricate dynamics of their role and nurturing healthy relationships with colleagues and communities alike.

Increasing self-awareness is a continuous process, not a one-time event. Understanding emotional intelligence includes researching the subject and utilizing tools that promote reflection. Writing in journals, meditation, and seeking advice from mentors and peers are all outlets for understanding personal feelings, biases, and opportunities for progress.

Imagine a map: you need to know your starting point before you can navigate to your destination. Similarly, you must acknowledge your current state before envisioning the officer you want to become. Self-reflection is the compass for this journey. It provides the clarity to identify areas for growth, allowing you to shed unproductive behaviors and embrace positive changes.

Feedback: The Key to Progress

Ken Blanchard aptly stated, "Feedback is the breakfast of champions." Constructive feedback from trusted colleagues and mentors is invaluable. Surround yourself with people who can give you honest feedback on your behavior. I call them eagles. These people serve as mirrors, reflecting reality as it is. They are the individuals who encourage you, point out your flaws, and celebrate your accomplishments.

Self-Reflection is Key

Throughout your journey in policing, you have undoubtedly picked up habits, both positive and negative, that shape your interactions with the community. Perhaps, over time, you've noticed a creeping robotic demeanor or a sense that all calls are just a repetitive routine. This is natural but can hinder your growth as an officer. Self-reflection can rekindle your excellence by helping you recognize your current state and guiding you towards becoming a better version of yourself.

In the demanding world of law enforcement, routine can unknowingly turn into complacency. The "same ol' shit, different day" mentality can diminish your enthusiasm and effectiveness. This is where self-reflection comes in; it's a crucial practice that allows you to step back and observe your actions, thoughts, and emotions objectively. Only by understanding where you are now can you chart a path to improvement.

Cultivating Positive Habits

Excellence thrives when negative habits are replaced with positive ones. You'll notice patterns that need to be changed as you participate in self-reflection. Utilize your self-awareness to reconnect with your community. Treat each interaction as a one-of-a-kind opportunity to rekindle your dedication to service and empathy. Protect yourself from allowing complacency. It can be an unwanted friend in the ever-changing landscape of police.

Yet, the power to change resides within you. By embarking on journeys of self-reflection and pursuing personal growth, you can navigate the challenges of policing with resilience, empathy, and an unwavering dedication to serving and safeguarding your communities.

Personality Types

Have you ever wondered which personality type is best for policing? Policing is complex and involves a wide range of tasks, responsibilities, and interactions with the public. Consider this -different personality traits may be advantageous in different situations.

Type A personalities, characterized by high achievement, competitiveness, and impatience, may possess traits that can be beneficial in certain aspects of policing. These individuals may be driven, focused, and determined, which could help them handle high-pressure situations, make quick decisions, and maintain a strong work ethic.

Type B personalities, on the other hand, with their easygoing, relaxed, and flexible nature, may excel in situations that require a calm and composed demeanor. They may be better at building rapport with individuals in the community, defusing tense situations, and demonstrating empathy and patience.

Type C personalities, who are accurate, rational, and logical, may bring valuable analytical skills to policing. They could be adept at gathering and processing information, conducting thorough investigations, and applying critical thinking to solve complex problems.

Congratulations, you have the right personality type. The ideal police officer may have a mix of traits from several personality types. It is crucial to emphasize that a person's potential to be a good police officer is not determined solely by personality attributes. Other aspects that influence an officer's effectiveness include training, experience, and communication skills. So, be you and improve where necessary.

CHAPTER 26
WE ARE OUR BROTHER'S AND SISTER'S KEEPER

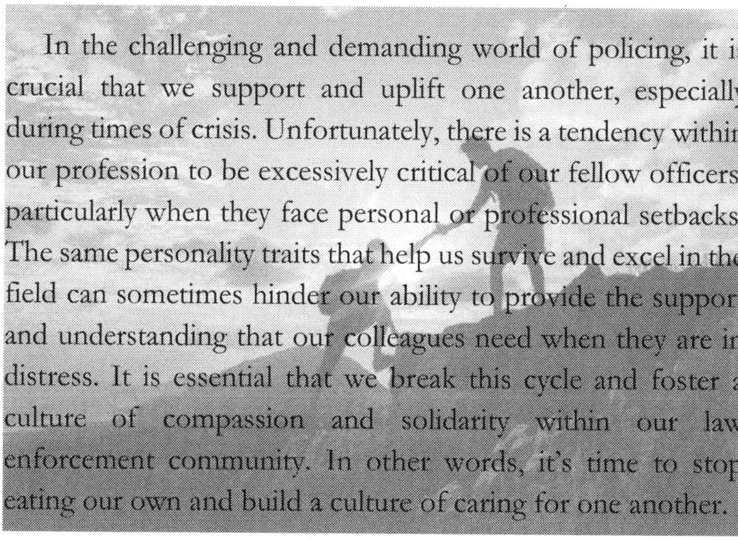

In the challenging and demanding world of policing, it is crucial that we support and uplift one another, especially during times of crisis. Unfortunately, there is a tendency within our profession to be excessively critical of our fellow officers, particularly when they face personal or professional setbacks. The same personality traits that help us survive and excel in the field can sometimes hinder our ability to provide the support and understanding that our colleagues need when they are in distress. It is essential that we break this cycle and foster a culture of compassion and solidarity within our law enforcement community. In other words, it's time to stop eating our own and build a culture of caring for one another.

ID178142279 © Nathanael Kiefer |Dreamstime.com

The Cost of Alienation

When one of our own experiences a crisis, whether it be in their personal life or on the job, it is disheartening to witness how they can be ostracized and isolated instead of receiving the support they need. We must recognize that these officers are not damaged goods but individuals who may be experiencing rough patches in life. It is our responsibility to be there for them, offering empathy and understanding, rather than perpetuating a culture of judgment and rejection.

The Impact of Competitive Traits

The same competitive traits that drive us to succeed in the field can sometimes contribute to a toxic environment within our ranks. Our ultra-competitiveness can lead us to view our colleagues' struggles as a sign of weakness or failure, rather than as an opportunity to extend a helping hand. It is important to acknowledge that we all face challenges, both professionally and personally, and that no one is immune to the trials and tribulations of life. Life will hit you hard at some point. Use your competitiveness towards being the best at lifting your brothers and sisters up whether it's to cheer them on for success or pulling them up from the valley to the mountain top.

Recognizing Our Shared Humanity

To foster a culture of support and empathy, we must acknowledge and embrace our shared humanity. Remember that underneath the uniform, we are all human beings. Police officers are not impervious to the difficulties that life presents. Divorce, mental health struggles, financial burdens, personal losses family issues, financial problems, and personal crises can impact any one of us. By breaking the stigma and opening discussions about these challenges, we can create an environment where officers feel comfortable seeking assistance without fear of judgment or retribution.

Life hits us hard, even while we are busy helping others through their own crises. Instead of turning a blind eye or pretending these issues do not exist, let's come together and provide the support and resources needed. We can build networks, peer support programs, and mental health initiatives to ensure that our colleagues have the tools to navigate life's challenges successfully.

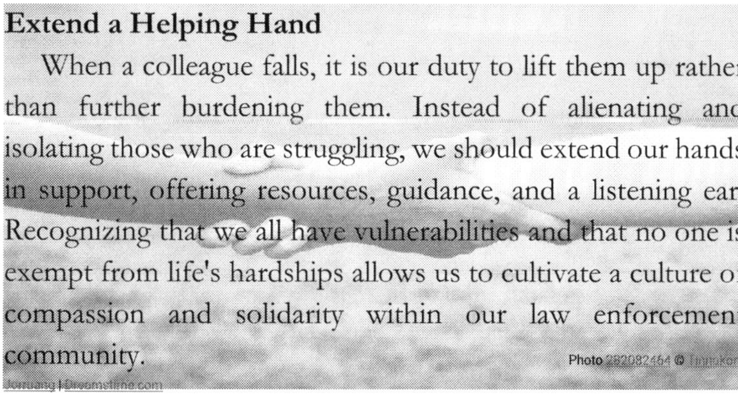

Extend a Helping Hand

When a colleague falls, it is our duty to lift them up rather than further burdening them. Instead of alienating and isolating those who are struggling, we should extend our hands in support, offering resources, guidance, and a listening ear. Recognizing that we all have vulnerabilities and that no one is exempt from life's hardships allows us to cultivate a culture of compassion and solidarity within our law enforcement community.

Changing the Narrative

It is time to shift the narrative within our profession. We must stop pretending that everything is always okay and acknowledge the realities of our humanness. By breaking the silence and destigmatizing the challenges we face, we create an environment where seeking help is encouraged and supported. This change starts with each one of us, recognizing our own biases and judgments and actively working to love and encourage our fellow officers.

Embracing a Culture of Compassion

Let's embrace a culture of compassion and empathy. This means actively listening to our colleagues, offering a helping hand without judgment, and providing a safe space for open dialogue. By setting aside competitiveness and embracing a collective mindset, we strengthen our bonds and create a supportive community where officers can thrive both personally and professionally.

Let's recognize the power we hold to positively impact the lives of our colleagues. Let's strive to be better, to embrace instead of tearing each other down. By welcoming our shared humanity, extending empathy, and actively supporting one another through life's challenges,
we can foster a law enforcement community that is resilient, compassionate, and united. It's time to stop eating our own and start building a culture of care and understanding within our ranks. Together, we can create a profession that not only serves and protects our communities but also uplifts and supports our fellow officers.

CHAPTER 27
RISE ABOVE NEGATIVITY

In the face of negativity and hate towards the police, it can be tough to maintain your focus. I want you to know you are not alone. As a police officer, you are a professional, and you are doing what's right. Don't let the opinions of others drag you down. Instead, I encourage you to channel that energy into being the best police officer you can be.

As difficult as it can be at times, treat people with respect, kindness, and humility, but always stay vigilant. Your duty is to protect and serve, and that responsibility should never be compromised. Support people when they want to exercise their right to express themselves under the first amendment. These days everyone is a reporter, maintain a sense of detachment from any negativity that comes your way. Do not get into a debate whether they are legit media or now, it really doesn't matter anymore. Don't take the bait from the few with a camera that want to show you in a negative light.

Avoid arguing with them, as it rarely leads to positive outcomes. It's best to give them as little attention as possible. If you receive a call about one of them, do your job but do not waste your time and energy in trying to "win' an argument. Get the facts and press on. Just like you've heard, "If you have a case, file it." If you don't, it's on to the next call. None of this is worth your frustration and energy. Keep your composure and professionalism, knowing that maintaining a calm demeanor portrays strength and authority.

By focusing on your purpose and conducting your duties with professionalism, you will find that most negative influences will fade away. Move forward with determination, conduct your business efficiently and effectively. If someone crosses the line and hinders your ability to serve, take appropriate action, but avoid getting tangled in unnecessary confrontations.

Remember, engaging in pointless battles only depletes your mental and emotional strength. Instead, be smart and strategic in managing difficult situations. Establish clear physical boundaries, such as using caution tape to secure a scene, and you will find that most will be less likely to test your limits. In your interactions with the public, be reasonable, patient, and understanding, all while keeping your safety at the forefront. By demonstrating these qualities, most people will support you when you need to act against those who refuse to cooperate.

Above all, be true to yourself. Show the world the incredible professional that you are, capable of handling challenges with wisdom and grace. Embrace your role as a police officer, knowing that your dedication to making a positive difference is far more significant than any negativity thrown your way. I know that with positivity and resilience, you will continue to shine as a beacon of hope in your community. Keep your head high, keep your focus sharp, and keep making the world a better place, one encounter at a time.

CHAPTER 28
CYNICISM, SARCASM, EMPATHY, AND GRACE

Cynicism: It's a curious thing – the longer you're in law enforcement, the more cynicism creeps in. That enthusiastic and optimistic version of yourself you once were seems to fade away. What gives? I remember a top-level commander once saying, "Policing would be a fantastic job if it weren't for the people!" And honestly, we get it. Screenwriter Lillian Hellman once noted, "Cynicism is an unpleasant way of saying the truth." But here's the twist – what's the truth, really? Maybe cynicism is a way of expressing partial truths because there's often some reality in it. As police officers, it's crucial to constantly challenge our own perception of truth.

Cynicism can be like a toxin that slowly seeps into our mindset. It's born out of repeated exposure to challenging situations, the feeling of being let down, and sometimes just sheer exhaustion. You've likely seen your fair share of difficult cases, uncooperative individuals, and the darker aspects of human behavior. Over time, it's easy to start viewing every situation through a cynical lens.

But here's the danger: cynicism can erode your motivation, your empathy, and your ability to truly connect with the people you're meant to serve and protect. It's like wearing a pair of glasses that tint everything in shades of doubt and disbelief. When you approach every situation with a cynical attitude, you're less likely to see the potential for positive outcomes. You might be quick to assume the worst intentions from others, even when they might genuinely need your help.

And let's not forget, cynicism spreads quickly. When you bring that negative attitude into your interactions with colleagues, it can poison the overall work environment. It becomes a self-fulfilling prophecy – if you expect people to be difficult or uncooperative, your behavior might unknowingly provoke those very reactions.

So, how do we combat this pitfall? Again, self-awareness is key. Recognize when cynicism is creeping in and challenge those negative assumptions. Try to see situations from multiple angles and always consider the possibility of positive outcomes. Surround yourself with colleagues who uplift and inspire you rather than perpetuating negativity.

Remember, the decision to be cynical or not is in your hands. It's easy to become jaded, but it takes strength to resist that path. In a profession that demands empathy, trust, and understanding, fighting cynicism is a necessary battle for both your own well-being and the effectiveness of your service.

The Sting of Sarcasm: If you've been married for more than a week, you're aware that sarcasm can be a real stinger. The truth is, sarcasm can be incredibly hurtful, especially when it's directed at you by someone you care about and trust. The saying "sticks and stones may break my bones, but words will never hurt me" is bullshit – words do hurt, especially when they come from a loved one or someone you trust.

As time goes on, many officers seem to develop a penchant for sarcasm. It might be a coping mechanism in the face of the daily grind. Police officers tend to have thick skin, so it might seem like joking around with fellow officers is harmless.

However, even with your colleagues, sarcasm has a way of piercing through that tough exterior.

But here's the crucial point: being sarcastic with citizens is never appropriate. One definition of sarcasm is "a sharp and often satirical or ironic utterance designed to cut or give pain."[xxxiii] It's no wonder it feels like a knife when you experience it. King David's words in Psalms 59:7 (NIV) capture the sentiment: "See what they spew from their mouths – the words from their lips are sharp as swords."[xxxiv] Your words carry more weight than you may think.

The etymology of the word "sarcasm" is enlightening. The first part, 'sarc' or 'sarx,' in Greek signifies tearing of the flesh. I know, it's a bit like the dad from the movie "My Big Fat Greek Wedding," but it's intriguing. The second part, '-casm' or 'chasm,' implies a deep divide or separation. So, sarcasm is essentially a tearing of the flesh that causes a profound separation. Okay, I've belabored the point, but you get the idea – sarcasm is meant to be painful.

Now, let's place ourselves in the citizen's shoes who has been on the receiving end of a sarcastic remark from a police officer. If people see the police as a legitimate authority, can you see how sarcasm can erode the trust the public places in you? Sarcasm can chip away at our efforts to gain trust and confidence. On top of that, sarcasm will only lead to trouble. It can damage your career, your department, and your community's perception of law enforcement.

Empathy: It's important to recognize that sympathy and empathy are two distinct realms. As aptly put by a fellow writer,

"Sympathy is feeling compassion, sorrow, or pity for the hardships that another person encounters, while empathy is placing yourself in the shoes of another."

In the world of law enforcement, showing compassion is a critical community expectation. When engaging with citizens, officers should aim to express compassion more openly. This simple act goes beyond duty; it conveys your care, understanding, and the sincere willingness to serve.

Yet, there are instances when officers can display empathy where it's suitable. Let's be clear – this doesn't mean you need to shed tears or offer hugs to everyone you encounter. What it does mean is that it's perfectly acceptable to feel the communal pain when tragedy strikes your city.

ID145113335 © Rosa Walker Dreamstime.com

Expressing empathy doesn't have to be complicated. Attending a funeral or vigil service quietly, writing a heartfelt message, or even penning a handwritten letter to those who are hurting can make a difference. Reflect on this: when an officer is gravely injured or, God forbid, loses their life in the line of duty, the community rallies around in extraordinary ways. They share in our sorrow and grief, offering their unwavering support. It's the essence of community.

Conversely, when your city grapples with a heartrending event, why shouldn't your police department extend a hand of empathy to those in pain? Of course, officers should maintain professionalism, especially during trying times. However, some moments warrant more than just fulfilling a duty. Expressing empathy demonstrates that we, too, can walk in their shoes and bear the weight of their anguish. This is what true community looks like.

Grace: While I am no preacher, I've always found solace in acknowledging and express gratitude for the grace bestowed upon me by a higher power. For me, that is God. I recognize that I do not deserve His grace or mercy. God's grace is usually defined in the bible as undeserved favor. My life, like all, has been marked by imperfections and mistakes, reminding me that such grace is undeserved and yet ever-present.

I do believe grace has a place in policing. Grace reminds us that we are not the judge of others and corresponds with another one of Sir Robert Peele's 9 principles, "Police should always direct their attention strictly towards their functions and never appear to usurp the powers of the judiciary." We are protectors of people, not judges of them. That is someone else's job here on earth. And should you believe in God, then He will decide the ultimate judgement for our actions on earth.

"…grace has a place in policing."

In the realm of policing, where encounters with individuals who have committed grievous acts are common, the act of extending dignity and respect can be tough. Despite voicing our intentions, it's often a challenge to uphold these values in the face of adversity. Remarkably, this challenge extends even within our own ranks. How then, can officers give grace and mercy to those we encounter if we can't even extend it to each other? This notion prompts consideration of sharing this grace within our professional realm.

Our duty as police officers involves interacting with individuals from all walks of life, regardless of their circumstances. It's crucial to remember that we are not in the position to pass final judgment upon them; that role is designated elsewhere. Just as the principles of Sir Robert Peel guide our conduct, we must recognize that our role is to fulfill our duties and refrain from assuming the authority of the judiciary. Embracing this perspective requires drawing strength, for humanity's sake, longing for the grace and mercy needed to extend it to all those we serve and encounter.

Envision a world where grace prevails in every interaction. As police officers, we have the unique power to impart this grace to countless individuals we engage with daily, beginning with our brothers and sisters in blue, irrespective of their perceived worthiness. Ultimately, that judgment is not ours to make.

PARTING THOUGHTS

As we reach the end of this book, let's pause and reflect on the journey we've taken together. We've explored some of the challenges and opportunities that define our noble profession. Each chapter has been a steppingstone, guiding us towards a deeper understanding of what it means to strive for excellence in the realm of law enforcement.

In these pages, we've navigated through and recognized the power of relevance, the intricacies of procedural justice, the concept of being agile, and empathy in building bridges and embraced the importance of unity within our own ranks. We've learned that excellence isn't a destination but a mindset, a commitment to continuous growth, and an unwavering dedication to service.

The tools shared within these pages are your allies. Approach each encounter with an open heart, a clear mind, and a resolute commitment to upholding the values that define our profession. Just as you're tasked with keeping your community safe, remember to safeguard your own well-being. Seek support when needed, cultivate resilience, and never underestimate the power of camaraderie.

The world of policing is ever evolving, and your actions have the potential to shape perceptions, mend divisions, and inspire change. Never underestimate the impact of a kind word, a listening ear, or a reassuring presence. Every interaction, every decision, contributes to the legacy we leave behind.

In parting, carry these thoughts with you: Be steadfast in your principles, compassionate in your interactions, and relentless in your pursuit of excellence. Your role is vital, your impact immeasurable, and your potential limitless.

Thank you for dedicating your time to explore the pages of this book. May your every endeavor as a police officer be one of purpose, fulfillment, and positive change.

With profound gratitude and respect,

Andy

BIBLIOGRAPHY

[i] Narang, S. (2020, August 25). Shadow Organizations – Good, Bad and Ugly. Retrieved August 15, 2023, from https://www.linkedin.com/pulse/shadow-organizations-good-bad-ugly-sanjay-narang/.

[ii] *Flint Town, Episode 2.* (n.d.). Retrieved August 15, 2023,.
…" protecting and serving in an urban community is much more than crime-fighting, the burden placed on urban police is they have the power to either tear a city apart or help hold it together,"BrianWillingham

[iii] Cheetah agility more important than speed | science | AAAS. (n.d.). https://www.science.org/content/article/cheetah-agility-more-important-speed

[iv] Drodz, K. (n.d.). Cultivating an agile mindset. Retrieved August 15, 2023, from https://www.atlassian.com/agile/advantage/agile-mindset#:~:text=The%20agile%20mindset%20is%20a,incremental%20value%20to%20their%20customers.

[v] "Agile." Merriam-Webster.com Dictionary, Merriam-Webster, https://www.merriam-webster.com/dictionary/agile. Accessed 15 Aug. 2023.

[vi] Hughes, K. (n.d.). The Agile Manifesto, Explained. Retrieved August 15, 2023, from https://www.projectmanager.com/blog/agile-manifesto-explained.

[vii] Drumond, C. (n.d.). Is the Agile Manifesto Still a Thing? Retrieved August 15, 2023, from https://www.atlassian.com/agile/manifesto.

[viii] Qazi, I. (n.d.). 12 Agile Principles in 12 Sprints — Deep dive into Agile Manifesto. Retrieved August 15, 2023, from https://www.scalablepath.com/project-management/12-agile-principles.

[ix] Excellence Quotes. (n.d.). Retrieved February 11, 2018, from https://www.brainyquote.com/topics/excellence

[x] Zimring, F. E. (2009). *The great American crime decline.* New York: Oxford University Press.

[xi] BibleGateway. (n.d.). Retrieved February 11, 2018, from https://www.biblegateway.com/passage/?search=Philippians%2B3&ve

rsion=ESV strain forward

[xii] Scott, S. (n.d.). Excellence is a Habit: 7 Lessons from This Aristotle Quote. Retrieved August 16, 2023, from We are what we repeatedly do.

[xiii] Collins, J. (2011) Good to Great. New York, NY: HarperCollins Publishers Inc.page 247-248

[xiv] Collins, J. (2011) Good to Great. New York, NY: HarperCollins Publishers Inc. Page 71-72

[xv] Saad, L. (n.d.). Historically Low Faith in U.S. Institutions Continues. Retrieved August 16, 2023, from https://news.gallup.com/poll/508169/historically-low-faith-institutions-continues.aspx.

[xvi] Tyler, T. R. (2006). *Why people obey the law.* Princeton, NJ: Princeton University Press. P. 3-5

[xvii] "Authority." Merriam-Webster.com Dictionary, Merriam-Webster, https://www.merriam-webster.com/dictionary/authority. Accessed 16 Aug. 2023.

[xviii] (n.d.). Retrieved from http://www.thefreedictionary.com/delegate

[xix] (n.d.). Retrieved from https://www.academia.edu/7762939/Trust_in_the_Police_The_influence_of_procedural_justice_and_perceived_collective_efficacy p.4

[xx] Meares, Tracey L., "Norms, Legitimacy and Law Enforcement" (2000). *Faculty Scholarship Series.* 515. P. 40 http://digitalcommons.law.yale.edu/fss_papers/515

[xxi] Weisburd, D., & Braga, A. A. (2008). *Police innovation: contrasting perspectives.* Cambridge: Cambridge University Press. P. 254

[xxii] Tyler, T. R. (2006). *Why people obey the law.* Princeton, NJ: Princeton University Press. P. 4

[xxiii] Weisburd, D., & Braga, A. A. (2008). *Police innovation: contrasting perspectives.*
Cambridge: Cambridge University Press. P. 253

[xxiv] Weisburd, D., & Braga, A. A. (2008). *Police innovation: contrasting perspectives.*
Cambridge: Cambridge University Press.

[xxv] Respect. (n.d.). Retrieved February 13, 2018, from https://www.merriam-webster.com/dictionary/respect

[xxvi] Yahoo Health. (2015, June 18). Science Reveals How to Make Yourself Appear More Trustworthy. Retrieved February 13, 2018, from https://www.yahoo.com/beauty/science-reveals-how-to-make-yourself-appear-more-121846659297.html

[xxvii] Legitimacy and Procedural Justice: A New Element of Police Leadership A Report by the Police Executive Research Forum (PERF). (2014, March(P.8). Retrieved February 13, 2018, from http://www.policeforum.org/assets/docs/Free_Online_Documents/Leadership/legitimacy%20and%20procedural%20justice%20-%20a%20new%20element%20of%20police%20leadership.pdf

[xxviii] BADGE OF LIFE FAQS. (n.d.). Retrieved February 13, 2018, from http://www.badgeoflife.com/badge-life-faqs/

[xxix] (n.d.). Retrieved from http://www2.cambridgema.gov/CityOfCambridge_Content/documents/Cambridge%20Review_FINAL.pdf P. 21

[xxx] (n.d.). Retrieved from http://www2.cambridgema.gov/CityOfCambridge_Content/documents/Cambridge%20Review_FINAL.pdf P. 3

[xxxi] n.d.). Retrieved from http://www2.cambridgema.gov/CityOfCambridge_Content/documents/Cambridge%20Review_FINAL.pdf P. 4

---

xxxii Department of Justice. (n.d.). Police Discretion. Retrieved August 16, 2023, from https://ojp.gov/ncjrs/virtual-library/abstracts/police-discretion-2#:~:text=However%2C%20since%20the%20Terry%20decision,should%20use%20increasingly%20wide%20discretion.

xxxii Sarcasm. (n.d.). Retrieved February 13, 2018, from http://www.merriam-webster.com/dictionary/sarcasm

xxxii Staff, B. (n.d.). Psalms 59:7 - see what they spew from their mouths-the words fr... biblestudytools.com. https://www.biblestudytools.com/psalms/59-7.html

ABOUT THE AUTHOR

Andy Harvey is a seasoned leader with a background in both military and law enforcement professions. Harvey retired as the First Sergeant of the 136th Mission Support Group in Ft. Worth, Texas. He served in support of Operation Iraqi Freedom and led in New Orleans days after the devastation of Hurricane Katrina.

Harvey attended the Non-Commissioned Officer Academy and First Sergeant Academy where he earned the Distinguished Graduate Award and the revered Commandant's Leadership Award, respectively. Harvey also retired from the Dallas Police Department where he held various commanding roles overseeing patrol, investigations, community relations, and media relations. As Chief of Police in various cities, Harvey introduced innovative programs and spearheaded policy changes that embraced forward-thinking approaches in policing.

Harvey earned a Master of Science degree in Criminal Justice from the University of North Texas. Furthermore, he is a graduate from the prestigious Senior Management Institute for Policing (SMIP), Texas Leadership Command College (LCC), the Caruth Police Institute (CPI), and the Institute for Law Enforcement Administration (ILEA).

Harvey authored his first book titled "Excellence in Policing," which resonated with police officers across the nation. He has been featured on local and national news programs to share his perspective on today's policing. Harvey's passion continues to inspire others and shape the future of policing.

Made in the USA
Columbia, SC
12 June 2025

b7535720-a578-4e53-9dfa-b767a0721dc8R01